CW01511459

THE SUMI

A History From Beginning To End

BY

HENRY FREEMAN

Table of Contents

Introduction

The way we make sense of the world, how we build our communities and societies, and how we interact with one another raise the question for many of us: how different are we from ancient civilizations? So many aspects of our daily lives can be traced back thousands of years to the cradle of civilization in the Middle East where the Sumerians lived for several millennia alongside other civilized groups. One of the earliest urban agrarian societies to emerge in the world in recorded history, the Sumerians left us with extraordinary answers to these questions in our efforts to understand how humans survived and progressed in various endeavors and how ancient human ideas shaped our world today.

The answers they left for us lie deep in the ground of ancient Mesopotamia. They have intrigued scholars and the curious reading public who try to piece together what life was like through each fragment that archaeologists have found and continue to find. These clay tablets, geological records, inscriptions, and cultural artifact traditions give us deeper meaning as we explore the development of the human race.

The extraordinary impact of their curiosity, skills, and discoveries on our everyday lives transcends the enormous amount of time that divides us from the Sumerians. Do you know if you had a chance to talk and have lunch with an ancient Sumerian today, they might be pleasantly surprised to know that we still keep time with their concept of a 24-hour day? All the devices we use to keep time might confuse them, but they'd be sure to appreciate that the system that we inherited from them still divides each hour into sixty minutes and each day into 24 hours. If you drew them a circle, they would know that it was 360 degrees all the way around, because they were the first to divide a circle into 60 degree sections some 4000 years ago. They used a base-12 system and a base-60 system rather than a base-10 system. The year was split into 12 segments. They used the base-60 system to divide a circle into 360 degrees.

This book will delve deeper below the surface on these and many more Sumerian contributions that help us make sense of the world, help u build our communities and societies, and help us interact with each other. It will show us of our similarities as well as our differences. It will trigger our imaginations; it will allow us a look through the extraordinary eyes of archaeologists, anthropologists, historians, and scholars as they continue to solve humankind's biggest mysteries.

At times, many of us get consumed by the worldview of our individual societies today and only see the Middle East as an area of the world that is distant, dangerous, and deeply embroiled in conflict. Over the years, teams of scientists have had to postpone excavations when world wars or regional conflicts would mean risking their lives. Now, in the meantime, many of us who read about Syrian refugees fleeing from their homeland, and who are just as concerned about the development of the human race, try to gain a better understanding of the nature of the conflicts in this region.

It's informative to place the problems in the region that we see today into a deeper historical and geographical context to guide us in developing a broader perspective and to appreciate their human struggles. With that in mind, it might surprise many that the disappearance of water and natural resources in the region is also related to ancient Sumerians. The very knowledge that they passed down to those generations who have tried to continue to live in the Fertile Crescent of Mesopotamia is being threatened. This book will open your eyes and reveal efforts to restore and retain the knowledge, practices, and plant life that hold historical and regional value.

In the race to save antiquities, the story of what impact the Sumerian civilization has had on us—despite the ages and our advancements—is irreplaceable. We see the incalculable importance of furthering our understanding at a time when we are witnessing the intentional destruction of the shared inheritance of different empires and civilizations by rogue violent groups like Daesh (ISIS). As we embark on this journey, we will learn about the resilience, values, culture, history, and kingdoms of the ancient Sumerians that drove this civilization to new heights. The ancient Sumerians continue to fascinate us and fill us with a sense of wonder despite their fall.

In honor of the importance the Sumerians placed on the number 12, the pages that lie between each of the following 12 chapters will intrigue you, raise more questions and provide some answers. As the clock ticks and the hours pass, our human thirst for knowledge to seek answers and achieve progress reveals the mastery and importance of these ancient people to the development of human civilization.

Chapter One

How We Know What We Know About Sumerians

Piecing together ancient remnants involves a high level of effort in the search for evidence. Historians, archeologists, cultural anthropologists and geologists have done most of the literal dirty work by unearthing an increasingly higher number of clues about the fascinating lives of the Sumerians. Among these source materials are thousands of clay tablets, inscriptions, architectural ruins, brick molds, tools, columns, sculptures, art, , metals, steles and cylinders. They've used carbon-14 dating for stratigraphic and dating purposes and various other techniques mentioned further in this chapter.

The evidence researchers have unearthed includes the infamous all-important King List, which is a 4,000-year-old unique cuneiform tablet found in the early 1900s at the site of ancient Nippur and published in 1906. It was written circa 2100 BCE and has proven to be an invaluable tool for establishing political and societal insights based on its list of rulers, Sumerian myths, legends, and hyperbolic accounts linking the kings to their gods. It reflects old traditions within a chronological framework that has provided both answers to existing questions while raising new ones altogether, and it explains how kingship was a divine institution to the Sumerians. Its influence on other Sumerian aspects of politics and society has been traced; as you will learn in the following pages, the pantheistic Sumerians were deeply motivated by pleasing their gods and had a complex system of deities that determined much of their fate.

The history of Sumer has been deduced from the accumulation of this tremendous amount of archeological, historical and geological evidence. Often, newer excavations are based on the knowledge of previous ones. Time will tell, as the saying goes, but what time has delivered to us is a growing understanding of the history of the Sumer people and their city-states. These city-states were in a state of near-constant warfare as they vied for control of the region. Time has shown many of their incredible inventions and systems, and will continue to present us with further knowledge with every new excavation. Famous Sumerologists include Samuel Noah Kramer and Thorkild Jacobsen, among many other historians and scholars that have shared fascinating accounts and interpretations of the evidence that the Sumerians left behind. Jacobsen in particular is known for offering those who study ancient Mesopotamian civilization hope for more collaborative research in the field; since its inception in the nineteenth century, the field recognized that the division of labor between archaeologists and historians has often skewed the end result of research.

Recordings from excavations go back to the 1600s. In fact, historians knew nothing about the Sumerians less than a century ago, because previously all excavations were looking for Assyrian historical artifacts, according to

Kramer. The discovery of the Sumerians came unexpectedly, which led to controversies. As the community interested in these ancient findings slowly embraced the concept that the Sumerian people from 6,000 years ago that resided in southern Mesopotamia were not the same as the Semitic [1] Akkadians or Babylonians, both from northern Mesopotamia, the key findings led to a major rediscovery of the Mesopotamian civilizations. It is important to note that in analyzing the artifacts and evidence, the accuracy of dates cannot be claimed with absolute certainty. However, all the citations referenced in assembling this primer attempt to provide the most commonly indicated dates for the various periods addressed throughout the Fertile Crescent region.

To put it in perspective, it turned out that the Sumerian Empire (circa 5000-2000 BCE) predated the Akkad Empire (circa 2400-2200 BCE), the Babylonian Empire (circa 1950-1600 BCE), the Kassite Empire (circa 1550-1100 BCE), and the Assyrian Empire (circa 1400-612 BCE) in the Mesopotamian (modern day Iraq) region. It's worth mentioning that a universally accepted chronology for the entire ancient Near East remains to be established. However, several reliable studies of world civilizations suggest that after the end of the last Ice Age in 15,000-10,000 BCE and the first evidence of agriculture, the Sumerians arrived in Mesopotamia circa 5000 BCE. The early history of Mesopotamia under the Sumerians includes great cultural and technological advances. All of the Mesopotamian empires were largely collections of city-states with the one city with the best army determining domination in the region, until the decline of Mesopotamia in the first millennium BCE, when King Cyrus II (Cyrus the Great) conquered Mesopotamia by 539 BCE.

Although Neolithic man experimented with copper tools and weapons, and every civilization went through its own Stone Age, Bronze Age, and then Iron Age, it wasn't until the fourth millennium BCE that tin was added to copper to produce the superior alloy, thus beginning the Bronze Age. The development of bronze in this region first occurred in Mesopotamia when the Sumerians discovered adding tin to copper could create bronze circa 3500 BCE. Since Sumer is considered the earliest known civilization, many researchers have found the application of their chemical knowledge astonishing. Sumerian texts found in Fara, Iraq dating to the middle of the third millennium BCE contain the earliest references to tin and bronze, with copper imported from Armenia in the Caucasus Mountains. Analysts have corroborated with textual evidence that bronze was being made in the region at that time. As you will read later, this alloy led to stronger weapons.

Before delving into the extraordinary traces of Sumerian life left for us to consider, the various interpretations of this evidence and their relevant influences on our daily lives, a look behind the scenes at how excavators determined what belonged to the Sumerians can help. Significant excavations have taken place in some of the main city-states of ancient Sumer as far back as 1616, when the first brick was brought back to

Europe showing the iconic Sumerian system of writing, cuneiform. We will explore this system of writing in the chapters ahead. In 1869, the French-German Assyriologist Jules Oppert correctly named the non-Semitic people who invented cuneiform at a lecture that he delivered to the French Society of Numismatics and Archeology, with the name "Sumerian" being the one applied by the Akkadians to the Semitic people of Assyria and Babylonia.

While the matter remained controversial—even considered as an artificial invention by some scholars—the Sumerian people and their language were no longer buried and mislabeled Babylonians, Assyrians or Akkadians. Leaving no stone unturned, the Irish linguist Edward Hincks - who had published significant contributions focusing on deciphering Akkadian script - had publicly expressed doubt in 1850 about the general assumption that the Semitic inhabitants of Assyria and Babylonia had invented cuneiform. This doubt was validated when excavations in the later 1870s and throughout 1880s solidly put the Sumerians on the map.

Figuring out where the Sumerians came from and why they settled in the region has led to years of discussions and analysis of settlement patterns of earliest known residents of this region. The study of changing settlement patterns of the times suggests that after the Ubaid period (circa 650 to 3800 BCE), which was characterized by small settlements by the semi-nomadic Ubaid people and some degree of site planning, the Sumerians came from the north or east, settled in the southern Mesopotamia region, and were the first to completely depend on irrigation systems. Therefore, one of the main distinctions that differentiated them from the Ubaid was that the Sumerians were no longer nomadic; instead, once the development of sophisticated irrigation systems, irrigation availability became the decisive factor in the location of city-states and agricultural sites.

It is a commonly accepted view that the earliest evidence of settlement in Sumer suggests that the urbanization that took root as a result of the Sumerian irrigation canals during the Uruk period necessitated cooperation. Irrigation led to the foundations for organized societies and cities, but it also led to the salination and later degradation of the soil. By 3500 BCE, Uruk had grown into a city with a population of 50,000. Since our knowledge about the Sumerians has become more extensive than of the Ubaid and other Mesopotamian people, scholars are still piecing together other important contributions to these historical events.

The Sumerian cities have provided a treasure of spectacular proportion to excavators lucky enough to discover these significant human contributions. While the cities of Ur and Uruk are considered the first Sumerian city-states, there were twelve separate city-states altogether: Kish, Erech (Uruk), Ur, Sippar, Akshak, Larak, Nippur, Adab, Umma, Lagash, Bad-tibira, and Larsa. Although this book will discuss the importance of these cities in terms of geography and dynasties later, knowing the names of the cities helps us understand the choice of excavation points throughout efforts to gain a better foothold on the ancient culture. In addition to these city-states, excavated materials first emerged from the ruins of Nineveh at the site of a royal library in the 1850s.

Although Nineveh was not a Sumerian city-state, it was however an ancient Akkadian city-state and the capital of the Assyrian Empire at its height. The royal mid-seventh-century library belonged to King Assurbanipal of Assyria, and while the Akkadian-speaking Assyrians and Babylonians were as known to history as the Persians, the Sumerian language and people weren't even a footnote, yet. The king had accomplished one of his greatest historical achievements when he commissioned new editions of Sumerian and Akkadian literature to be housed at the largest library in ancient Mesopotamia. Thankfully, speculation about the different scripts found in these books at Nineveh opened to the possibility that bilingually written texts could include another real language.

This eventually led to the determination that this language was Sumerian, supported of course by mounting evidence of an older form of cuneiform than that of the Akkadians. Once linguists and Assyriologists began to wonder and ask more questions, they found the answer in an early Akkadian record found on the mysterious shelves of Nineveh in which the ancient kings called themselves "king of Sumer and Akkad". Soon, excavated tablets from the Early Dynastic period in southern Mesopotamia (Sumer) began to come to light and experts were able to verify and match the languages in both texts.

The 30,000 clay tablets written in cuneiform found in Nineveh are the single most important source of knowledge about ancient Mesopotamia and have contributed significantly to our understanding of the almost overlooked pioneering Sumerians and trade during their time. Since the ores needed to make copper required refinement in order to rid the metal of its waste products, removing the waste material reduced the weight of raw copper and allowed merchants to ship larger loads back to Sumer. Their cultural commitment to trade showed how vital control of production of bronze was to their way of life. They worked with local nomads, who were often migrant in nature, to provide required labor. Some gave up their hunting and gathering or herding lifestyles to work in Sumerian mines or commodity production sites. Reciprocal relationships relied on a continued buoyance of the Sumerian culture.

The large role that excavations have had in the Sumerian cities mentioned cannot be taken lightly given the amount of evidence that has contributed to our greater understanding of Sumerian life and contributions to modern living. Although there are books dedicated to listing every excavation, those mentioned in this primer will hopefully lead you, the reader, to further your own exploration. The pages that follow will reveal the results of many of these excavations based on what aspect of life the evidence has improved in our struggle to grasp the life and times of the Sumerians.

Additionally, there are a number of noninvasive methods and traditional surveys, supplemented by a host of remote-sensing techniques that use innovative technologies like satellite imagery, ground-penetrating radar, digital imaging, computer modeling, and magnetometry to probe historical sites called *tells*, which literally means "mounds" in Arabic, and designates a typical archeological site. These archaeological projects also include natural scientists drawing together soil scientists, climatologists, botanists, and volcanologists to work with archeologists to help explain climate change and societal collapses in the Early Bronze Age in Mesopotamia.

Chapter Two

The Bronze Age – Sumer And Its Contemporaries

What's the best advice you can give yourself whenever you put money down on the table? That's right: write it down. That wasn't just something you learned from college, high school, the family negotiator or your first misunderstanding over a sale or service. Based on evaluations of clay tablet documents, trade may have been the main motivator for the Sumerians to develop a system of writing initially. Many of the clay tablets that have been found are of a business nature. The Sumerian Bronze Age began in 3150 BCE when far-ranging trade networks were established. Archeologists distinguish among the Early Bronze Age (3500-2000 BCE), Middle Bronze Age (2000-1600 BCE), and Late Bronze Age (1500-1200 BCE) for both the Northern and Southern Mesopotamia. During the Early Bronze Age, writing truly emerged as a major data source; however, written evidence is fragmentary and often provides a partial perspective, even as it informs our understanding of their past.

This age marked a time of demographic flux in the Mesopotamian region. Conflicts between nomads, emerging cultivating zones and city-states, expansionism and political centralization all characterized this era and region. It was mostly patchworks of relatively autonomous city-states, although given the sources from the Mesopotamian region, there were conflicts with nomadic cultures in the area. There are numbers of bills of sale, receipts, and documents that, upon further investigation, reveal that the Sumerians documented their economic production using a specific pictographic writing that had more than 2,000 shapes. The sheer volume caused confusion; as a result Sumerians began to develop cuneiform script. The first written tablets in this proto-cuneiform are around 85% administrative or accounting in nature.

While there are many portrayals of the Mesopotamian region's rise of early civilizations, one thing that has harbored criticism is the notion that these first civilizations emerged as solo performances. In fact, from at least the middle of the fourth millennium, Mesopotamia experienced continuous contact with its surrounding indigenous cultures. Sumer itself was small at roughly 10,000 square miles - a little smaller than the modern country of Belgium, and while the chapter that focuses on trade will further investigate the nature of the trade relationship that explains the business clay tablets that have been excavated, a look at how Sumer and its contemporaries spread out both geographically and in terms of the Bronze Age Sumer experienced can be appreciated. While the extent and manner of the cultural contact and influence is the subject of vast volumes and debates, acknowledging the overlapping historical records of various groups during this Bronze Age can broaden our perspective of the past.

How do we know that ancient cultures were in communication with each other? Who was the communication with? For one thing, we know that there was contact during the Bronze Age that was established between Sumer and the Zagros or Caucasus, as foreign products were needed in most cases in the use of bronze. The abundance of exotic substances found in Sumerian graves and the discovery of seals that were manufactured in India demonstrate the success of and their dependence on foreign trade. It is also supported by the fact that distinctive archeological cultures along the Euphrates River, Central Asia and the Indus Rivers shared a common technique for the production of pottery and the manufacture of metal artifacts that developed over time. Before the Sumerian civilization began to organize itself as a city-state civilization with the use of irrigation, the Ubaid culture of the mid-fifth to late fourth millennium extended from the Arabian Peninsula and the Iranian shores of the Persian Gulf to northern Mesopotamia and western Iran.

There is considerable debate surrounding why they expanded, as mentioned in *The Sumerian World* by Harriet Crawford, who has published extensively on various topics surrounding the Sumerian civilization based on her own excavations and experience as an Honorary Visiting Professor in the Institute of Archeology, University College in London, UK. However, she explains that the Ubaid culture is treated as a foundational stage of the emergence of the Mesopotamian cultural complexity, and is seen as a complex chiefdom or an early state formation. The Ubaid culture was known to be profoundly different from the cultures of the Zagros Mountains and the Khuzistan steppes.

If pre-Iranian cultures that predate the Sumerians interacted with other cultures, did the Sumerians? In building an understanding of Sumerian culture and how in its bid as the earliest civilization it influenced and was influenced by other cultures, experts have studied Mesopotamian inscriptions and literary texts to get a general idea. It appears that Elam (the present day Khuzistan province of Iran) refers to the southeastern half of the highlands bordering on Mesopotamia near the Zagros Mountains. Subar (Subartu) is considered the area that generally covered the northeastern highlands to the north of Elam. At the time, these were not political entities, but general geographical terms. Elamites were heavily influenced by Sumer, yet they had a distinct language and were not politically part of Mesopotamia.

The relationship between Sumerians and Elamites is characterized as hostile, with warfare being pervasive, This debilitated trade crossing the Iranian plateau, and is blamed on the cultural divide that separated the two civilizations. Their shared cultural boundary dates back to the sixth millennium. Scholars have published greatly on the resistance to central authority by the tribes of the Zagros Mountains and the role of pastoral nomadism in regional conflicts that defined relations with city-state forming entities like Sumer.

If Elam marked the east boundary, then north of them were the Gutians, close to the Zagros Mountains. Further north was Assyria, including Anatolia (central Turkey) in the Northwest. To the west, there was the Arabian Desert and Egypt. Further northeast was Urartu, and to the east, over the Zagros Mountains, there was Parthia and the Iranian plateau. The Gutians were semi-nomads from the mountains that the Sumerians called subhuman barbarians. It is the Gutians who contributed to the fall of the Akkadian empire after the Akkadians conquered the Sumerians. The Gutian period is considered the dark ages of Sumerian history (2218-2047 BCE). There is more about the Gutian period and its conflicts later in Chapter 9.

Assyria became middleman between Sumer and Babylon in securing valuable mining deposits of the Anatolian Plateau, according to the "Origins of Globalization" by Karl Moore and David Charles Lewis. Meanwhile, in "Commerce and Colonization in the Ancient Near East" by Maria Eugenia Aubet, the Assyrians acquired copper at a good price from the Old-Assyrian colony of Durhumid and sold it to the main metallurgical centers in the region. According to this research, the Sumerians actually received their copper mainly from the Magan mines on the Persian Gulf, and the Assyrians were the intermediaries.

While the study of trade circuits is elaborate and reveals the complexity of piecing together the puzzles of ancient times, the Sumerians, in looking back at the times that predated the Bronze Age, reveled in their accomplishment of building up a city like Uruk. They did this to fulfill setting up exchange relations with neighbors who were richer in resources that improved the quality of their own lives.

An area of study that has broadened our perspective of the past is the origins of globalization. Remnants of the past shed light on relations between the kings of Sumer and Akkad, and in the bronze-eager markets of Sumer and Akkad awaiting wares from the mouth of the Indus. Luxury goods sailed westward on Sumerian boats. Trade between India and Sumer in the third millennium BCE was risky; according to Indian scholar Shareen Ratnagar, consignments of cargos between India and Mesopotamia were possibly made only once a year. While the Sumerians were the first urban civilization, their neighbor Egypt was considered in the Bronze Age the world's oldest coherent nation-state that emerged in the valley of the Nile.

While the Egyptian Fifth Dynasty ruled the Nile delta, the Sumerians were venerating different gods in each of their many city-states - unlike the Egyptian politically-centralized Old Kingdom, which reflected the supremacy of a single god. According to "Origins: The Ancient Near Eastern Background of Some Modern Western Institutions" by William Halo, the Egyptian great temple complexes were dedicated to the sun-god, *Re*, who was the major object of worship at the time. In Sumer, however, the temple complexes to individual gods designated for each city-state occupied a prominent place within each city, while Egyptian temple complexes were built in necropolises, or "cities of the dead", in the western desert. Still, the Egyptians were also worshiping *Hat-hor*, the

"Mistress of Dendera", with a number of priests serving both *Re* and *Hat-hor*.

The number of ideas that came from the Bronze Age and the Sumerian civilization, and the effects of its relationships with contemporary civilizations, is significant. Many historians believe that the Sumerian culture and civilization had penetrated as far east as India, as far west as the Mediterranean, as far north as the Caspian Sea, and as far south as Ethiopia. During the Bronze Age, given the Sumerian achievements of developing agricultural surpluses based on building irrigation and exportation and importation of goods beyond its borders, the Sumerians developed essential fundamental staples for human civilization to thrive. The bronze metallurgy that developed there is well attested to throughout the third millennium and all over the ancient world by the second millennium.

Historian Paul Johnson argues that when the strongly-unified Egypt was encouraged towards its rapid growth with the need to irrigate farmland and manage flooding, it was at this point that Egyptian history diverged from that of the other alluvial valley-plains such as the Tigris-Euphrates and the Indus. It bypassed the city-state phase that was the impetus for trade and commerce in Sumer, according to "The Origins of Globalization" by Karl Moor and David Charles Lewis. Still, the core of the early Bronze and Middle Bronze system remained in Mesopotamia, and the struggle for control of the system made the Sumerian model dominant for 1,500 years.

Scholars that study metallurgy of the time consider that by 3000 BCE, Egyptian and Sumerian metallurgy comprised two distinct schools. Archaeologists distinguish between Egyptian weapons and Sumerian weapons, as well as other metal products. Some consider early Sumerian metallurgy superior to the contemporary Egyptian in extent and quality, according to "The Bronze Age" by V. Gordon Childe. However, much more thorough evaluations need to be made not only to support that claim, but also to address uncertainties surrounding whether Sumer or Egypt was the original center of metallurgy.

Akkadians and Eblaites developed their literate civilizations north of Sumer and were stimulated by Sumerian commercial and colonial activities. There is little evidence that there were struggles between the two groups early on, although both the Semitic Akkadians and the Sumerians did appear to experience subsequent rises and falls under various kings resulting from fierce battles between them. (More about how the Akkadians conquered the Sumerians in 2334 BCE and the subsequent fall of the Akkadians and reemergence of Sumer will be shared in Chapter 9.) However, for the purposes of establishing who the Akkadians and Eblaites were in the early Bronze Age, military experts consider that ancient Sumer and Akkad produced the most sophisticated armies of the Bronze Age. The ancient city-state of Akkad (now central Iraq) can be found 200 miles north of Sumer. Babylonia was called Sumer and Akkad at various times throughout the third millennium.

Architectural features found in Sumerian architecture have also been found in Babylonian monument architecture. Rapid expansion of Sumer was due to the extensive commercial ties and favorable geographic position they held.

As researchers point out, the history of the settlement patterns in the Mesopotamian plains is inextricably linked to its physical environment. Mapping the ancient settlements of Akkad and Sumer depends greatly on the sedimentation patterns of the Tigris and Euphrates. Since sedimentation in the region of the Ubaid and Uruk sites was less severe than in regions where the Akkad settled, it affects the extent of burial of the earliest sites. Historical geographies have however been constructed through survey data and landscape studies. However, patterns of settlement in Akkad are unreliable because of heavy alluviation. More therefore can be deduced about the urban origins at Uruk, the site of an urban explosion that experts have determined was one of the results of the social changes that led rural settlements and pastoral nomadic groups to favor cities.

The emergence of large urban centers like Ebla (modern day Syria) in northern Mesopotamia and Susa in Elam in the southeastern half of the highlands during the middle of the third millennium is recorded in numerous archival records. They show the extent of the use of writing to document these enterprising economies. The Eblaites based their economy on agriculture, viticulture, animal husbandry, and the metallurgical and textile industries. They did not mine their metal locally so they conducted trade with the Anatolians and maintained contact with kingdoms located in the region. Evidence of scribal practices has led experts to determine that Ebla was influenced by the Sumerian cuneiform tradition. Scholars have also considered that comparisons between northern and southern objects and palaces suggest that the north was not a backwater.

The prospect of intercultural exchanges and trade grew exponentially during this time. Some scholars like Samuel Noah Kramer characterize the relationship between Sumerians and their neighbors as one of give-and-take. When we study the history of the Bronze Age and the importance of understanding chemistry and applying it to improve the quality of life of humans throughout history, we find something extraordinary; according to "The Story of Chemistry" by N.C Datta, the Sumerian civilization that developed on the banks of the Tigris and Euphrates, the Egyptian civilization that developed on the banks of the Nile, and the Indus Valley civilization that grew on the banks of the Indus were tremendous in their achievements. During the entire period of their civilizations, they reveal a remarkable display of chemical knowledge in the form of pigments, pottery, metal-work, fabric, medical treatments and construction.

Evidence shows that after human civilization changed from the Stone Age to Neolithic with the discovery of copper mines in Egypt in 5000 BCE, humans had begun to use bronze, silver and gold by 4000 BCE. The Bronze Age started to collapse around 2500 BCE with the discovery of iron, since it was a much harder material than either copper or bronze. Studies that consider South Asia's first civilization, labeled Harappa by archaeologists, have shown that the Bronze Age in India led to a Harappan trade colony in Mesopotamia, and that trade may have been substantial in the 3rd millennium BCE. Sumerians traded with the Harappan civilization in the Indus Valley; Harappan seals have been found in the Sumerian city of Ur, suggesting trade between 2300 and 2000 BCE. According to "Societies, Networks, and Transitions: Volume I: A Global History" by Craig Lockard, Bahrain Island in the Persian Gulf functioned as a major crossroads for the Harappan-Sumerian trade.

While the nature of the relations that Sumer had with its neighbors can be more conveniently discussed within the framework of conflicts, regional domination, war and trade (which you will see later in this book), it is interesting to note that some scholars take a different approach to considering the intercultural ties that were established during these times. Gil Stein, author of "Rethinking World-Systems-Diasporas, Colonies, and Interaction in Uruk," sees the Uruk expansion into the Anatolian highlands during the fourth millennium BCE as less about Mesopotamians attempting to dominate the people of the distant periphery; instead of viewing them as colonizers in relations, they were more likely relying on the existence of a political, economic and social connectivity. They were recognizing the interdependence of cultures in Mesopotamia and at the periphery, which began in the Ubaid period, and were maintaining contact with "the other." This contact could be defined in various ways.

After the Ubaid period, the Sumerian expansion, also known as the Uruk expansion, occurred circa 4000-3100 BCE. As mentioned, Uruk drew many people from the rural regions, the explanation of which has become an area of study for those who examine settlement patterns and what led to the preponderance of city-states. Researchers say that Uruk may have been the largest city in Mesopotamia, if not the world, in 3200 BCE. Generally, the Uruk expansion into the area of Susa, east of Uruk in Elam, is generally interpreted as a colonial takeover. Uruk also expanded into Northern Syria and the Anatolia area in the Northern Highlands circa 3700 BCE. Material remains in numerous archaeological sites in these distant areas serve as evidence of these distant settlements that were established circa 3600 BCE. While experts continue to debate the reason the Sumerians built new settlements in foreign regions, the Uruk cultural expansion made it to Nineveh in the north, Suse in the east, and into the Anatolia area. When considering the striking discoveries of Syrian archeology, archaeologists have found the profusion of southern Mesopotamian-style material culture found across the Syrian landscape striking, according to "Archeology of Syria: From Complex Hunter-Gathers to Early Urban Societies" by Peter Akkermans and Glenn Schwartz.

Researchers also acknowledge the widespread debate of whether to read the Uruk expansion in terms of a full-scale colonial or imperial presence or in some other fashion. It's fascinating to consider the expansion and what archaeologists have identified as Uruk trading colonies, which were formed as an extensive interaction network connecting the southern Mesopotamia with the less urbanized neighboring areas. However, the question posed in publications focusing on the archeology of colonialism and cultural anthropology still remains: why did the Uruk expansion seem to have ended fairly abruptly in 3100 BCE with the abandonment or destruction of Uruk settlements in Syria, Anatolia and the Zagros mountain area?

The demand for raw materials, such as tin, copper, ivory and lapis sparked the development of far-reaching trade routes during the Middle Bronze Age.

Chapter Three

How Did The Sumerians Become Civilized?

If Sumerians in Mesopotamia began civilization on the Earth around 4500 BCE in the area of the Tigris and Euphrates Rivers, and Mesopotamia is considered the cradle of civilization and home to the forefathers of modern culture, then what makes humans civilized? Sumer is known as the land of civilized kings - what sets them apart from those who are not civilized? Does it have to do with leaving a rudimentary way of life and embracing ways to develop a higher quality of life? What exactly makes a people civilized? If the kings are civilized, does it mean a civilization is forming?

The Sumerians called themselves Sag-giga (the "black-headed" or "bald-headed" ones) and their southern Mesopotamia land *Kengi* ("civilized land") or Kengi-Sumer. Sumer is an Akkadian name, which means land of the civilized kings. According to "History in Black: African Americans in Search of An Ancient Past" by Yaacov Shavit, experts are ready to consider the possibility that the early population of Asia was black-skinned. Is that what the Sumerians meant by Sag-giga? Still, modern historians are divided on the identity of the early Sumerian culture and whether this is realistic or a figurative description. However, getting back to deciding how they came to consider themselves *Kengi* or "civilized land," what made them think they were civilized? They considered that civilization was a result of the gods' triumph over chaos. That seems to be one way that we consider being civilized.

At a Dialogue of Civilizations conference in Guatemala in 2013, archeologists discussed ancient cultures, the nature of civilization, and how to view the past as a window to the future. Archeologist Chris Thornton, the moderator of the panel, commented that the word "civilization" has become a loaded term that somehow implies that anything that is uncivilized is somehow bad or sub-human. To avoid that interpretation, they conference-goers presented an alternative definition: a culture becomes a civilization when it has various combinations of elements. These can include extensive food production, codified laws and administration, form of detailed writing, complex social roles, labor specialties and monumental architecture. However, Thornton, when thinking about the ancient Sumerians, brought up their epic of Gilgamesh, which may be known to many readers. In the epic, he said, the wildman Enkidu becomes civilized by participating in four distinct endeavors. Those endeavors include experiencing human love, putting on clothing, eating non-wild food, and playing sports. He suggests that that is quite a different definition than what civilization currently means.

As other possibilities of how we define civilization have been considered, the idea that civilization isn't necessarily the best option but instead a necessary one, especially when a growing population and limited resources can also reflect the reality of ancient times.

To understand better how the Sumerians became a civilization is to consider all of these possibilities and draw upon what was happening at the time. They became the first people to congregate in cities. They abandoned their tent-dwelling existence. They farmed. They built houses. They developed the first system of writing. They developed laws and codes that delineated rights of property and limited political authority. They constructed irrigation systems and drained canals and marshes. Their accomplishments in building up their city-states will be discussed further in Chapter 8; however, given the thought and planning it took to build their city-states - and their devotion to pleasing their gods - it's not surprising how they felt about founding their first city, the city of Eridu. In the Sumerian King's List, when the gods first gave human beings the gifts necessary to cultivate society, they applied those gifts and established the city of Eridu. Apparently, by establishing order, they had become a civilization in their own minds.

The Sumerian societal contributions of initiating attempts at becoming literate with some of the earliest known dictionaries in the world made them extremely important in studies focused on the origins of literacy. It is considered an indication of the initial civilizing process. Since they developed writing in the middle of the fourth millennium BCE and learned how to make tools and weapons before 3000 BCE, all of the subsequent and corresponding "firsts" continue to fascinate us and feed our curiosity and sense of wonder about the human experience. Their interest and commitment to becoming civilized despite the inherent challenges of geography and limited resources led to amazing accomplishments.

According to Samuel Noah Kramer in "The Sumerians: Their History, Culture, and Character," there is little doubt that they considered themselves a kind of "chosen people." In order to get into the ancient Sumerian mindset, he analyzed their myth "Enki and the World Order." The myth reveres the god Enki's ability to create and organize the natural and cultural entities and processes essential to civilized society. In the myth, he blesses Sumer, which showed that the Sumerians thought of themselves as a rather special and hallowed community intimately related to the gods.

Samuel Mercer in his eye-opening study of Sumerian morals in the "Journal of the Society of Oriental Research, Volumes 1-2"explores the idea that a sense of moral evil must go with a feeling of free will. He concludes that while Sumerian society, like every other society, is conditioned by social traditions, personal initiatives led to progressive strides in ancient civilization socially. In the case of the Sumerians, they emphasized the established nature of the family that made the father the leader of the family unit and social customs absolute. However, reforms and personal initiatives in family law and society at large did have a place in civilization, despite the systemic conditioning of the king or state being able to take actions based on heredity, environment, and tradition.

These moments in human evolution are interesting in the sense that despite how steeped in tradition or customs, the sense of morals of a people allowed for the civilization to preserve the customs while also allowing for personal initiative for social improvements that have been documented to occur through their civilization to improve the lives of those who may be considered inferior or secondary to the patriarch. "Ungendered Civilization" by K. Anne Pyburn mentions that the invisibility of women in archaeological record in studies of Mesopotamia's first civilization is caused by archaeologists' one-sided focus on temples and palaces. While women could become priestesses in Sumerian culture and worked in many industries, it is interesting to note that women in texts that focus on the context of political leadership played a nurturing role to strengthen the position of male rulers and heroes. Women did in fact not just live out traditional structural concepts of life since they were involved in physical work, engaged in business, testified in legal proceedings, and were protected by laws that allowed them to own property, as evidenced by archived clay tablets. Their roles were more diverse than has often been assumed and their personal initiative in building the civilization is not just to be conveniently wrapped into the loaded look at the past that has identified their civilization as a traditional society.

The division of labor and gender roles varied significantly in early civilizations according to "Understanding Early Civilizations: A Comparative Study" by Bruce Trigger. Some scholars consider the status of women a standard of civilization. With civilization came the beginning of social classes; these social classes were different in the cities than in rural tribal areas. In the cities, there were freemen, who did the bulk of the work and trading. Priests and noble landlords had a monopoly on the higher offices in the city. Slaves were numerous and often possessed various skills. The city was ruled by the elite, headed by the king. In villages, social equality was rarely challenged, while in the cities distinctions between people was essential and expected to be displayed in many fashions and activities. It affected the lives of both men and women and according to several scholars, Sumerian women had more rights than women in many later civilizations. The Sumerians were also very concerned with oppression of the poor by the wealthy and the living conditions of orphans and widows. All received legal protections and social norms advocated goodwill towards them.

Runners and scribes were well employed. Runners who delivered documents received land as part of their compensation if they were the king's runners. Many of the kings were literate, but they all had scribes. Kings and emperors set up inscriptions proclaiming their titles and chronicling their victories over enemies. Educated scribes could consider service to the palace, or temple, or as an accountant as job possibilities. Scribes went through a very thorough education as will be described in Chapter 10. In their early years, according to Harriet Crawford in "The Sumerian World," a scribe would seal documents using a seal that bore his name, but no title. Later, he would commission a new seal or recut the old one, to include the scribal title.

One might think that the standards of civilization would vary appropriately. Studies that compare Western civilization to Near Eastern ones like the Sumerians argue that even based on studying their literature, architecture, and crafts, one can see a considerable difference between what makes one a Western civilization and the other a Sumerian one. For instance, in "The Uniqueness of Western Civilization" by Ricardo Duchesne, the author argues that even when looking at Sumerian architecture and literature one can see the symbols of the subservience of man to the gods, and that the was the gods that were credited for the achievements of the Sumerian civilization. However, Western civilization celebrates tales of personal heroism among more individualized cultures of the West, which has led to foundational values and ideals of the West that celebrate the dawn of Western civilization in tales of such as The Iliad and Beowulf to name a few.

If all this makes you wonder what exactly is a civilization, good; the question is still an open one. Can there really be universal standards of law and civilization when there is a world of cultural diversity that reflect the norms of their times? After considering the economic, religious, and social structures, as well as the political and urbanizing forces at work during the Sumerian civilization that will be introduced in the following pages, continue debating this topic. The Sumerians did achieve an advanced state of human society and reached a high level of science, culture, industry and government. Based on some definitions, they were not bands (small groups of 25-60 individuals who were united based on some form of kin relationship). They were not tribes of a few hundred to a few thousand settled farmers or pastoralist herders, since they weren't loosely organized and had a strengthened control over their city-states with a social hierarchy. They were not organized into chiefdoms with over 10,000 individuals, since they didn't have chiefs, but kings. They were an agrarian civilization made up of approximately more than 60,000-100,000 individuals, comprising a complex society with social stratifications ruled by kings, and had entered the process of urbanization by creating the first city-states.

The very presence of Sumer as a civilization benefited the region and surrounding areas of Mesopotamia and developed an atmosphere willing to invest and generate advancements.

Chapter Four

How Long Were They Around

Geological evidence in a study entitled "the Geographical History of the Mesopotamian Plains" reveals that Sumer had been above water long before 4500-400 BCE. This explains why some archaeologists and cultural anthropologists think that it is possible that humans had settled there considerably earlier than generally assumed. Some consider that the lowest level of cultural remains in Sumer may still be inaccessible. It's possible, according to Samuel Noah Kramer in "The Sumerians: Their History, Culture and Character," that archeologists have been misled by higher water levels to believe they had been touching virgin soil.

As mentioned earlier, there is much speculation about the people who predate the Sumerians. Some scholars have called them the Proto-Euphrateans. In archeology, the Proto-Euphrateans are known as the Ubaid people, which were mentioned in Chapters 1 and 2. The Ubaid period was circa 5000-4100 BCE. Generally, it's accepted that the Sumerians came into the area where they settled in around 4500 BCE. They may have come from around Anatolia, in modern day Turkey. Their city-states thrived from about 3,000 BCE. As mentioned in a previous chapter, the Bronze Age began in 3150 BCE, when they established far-ranging trade networks, and ended in the area circa 1500 BCE. In 2350 BCE, King Sargon of Akkadia conquered all the Sumerian city-states and united them under his rule, creating the first Mesopotamian Empire. The Akkadians ruled Sumer for the next two centuries, while the cities revolted. The Semitization of Sumer began and ended the identifiable political and ethnic entity of Sumerian people.

The Akkadian Empire collapsed sometime after 2,200 BCE when the Gutians invaded. This is considered the Gutian period (2218-2047 BCE) and is also considered the Dark Ages of Sumerian History. The Imperial city of Ur revived Sumer when King Ur-Nammu in 2112 BCE founded the Third Dynasty of Ur. He ruled almost the whole of Sumer and Akkad. The Sumerian Renaissance that occurred during the Third Dynasty of the city of Ur after the collapse of the Akkadian Empire between 2047-1750 BCE brought a cultural revival to Sumer. King Ur-Nammu made cultural advancements a goal of his administration and maintained a peace so that the arts and technology could flourish. His son Shulgi's reign afterwards (2094-2047 BCE) lasted almost fifty years and made Ur the capital of an extensive empire. He also focused on cultural revival, although he further expanded Sumer by conquering lowland regions of the Zagros Mountains.

Sumerians were eclipsed in 1750 BCE by neighboring Semites when the Elamites and Amorites invaded. The Semitic Amorites, or Old Babylonians, conquered the plains under the Emperor Hammurabi in the 1700 BCE. He attributes being given the lands to *Anu*, the Supreme sky god, and *Bel*, the lord of heaven and earth and ruler of the destiny of the world in his letters.

"As for the land of Sumer and Akkad, I collected the scattered people thereof, and I procured food and drink for them. I pastured them, and I caused them to dwell in peaceful habitation."

—Emperor Hammurabi (from "The Letters and Inscriptions of Hammurabi, King of Babylon, about B.C. 2000")

When Hammurabi died in 1750 BCE, the empire disintegrated into small city-states ruled by weakened kings. The technologically-advanced Hittites, an Indo-European group of tribes, emerged out of modern-day Turkey and conquered Babylon. When they constructed their empire, it included the Zagros Mountains and Palestine. They took over Sumer about 1500 BCE. They pushed westward to Canaan. In "The Hittites and their Language" by Claude Reignier Conder, he concluded that the Hittites were a Mongol tribe that was finally scattered circa the seventh century BCE and that although their language was clearly Mongol, not Aryan or Semitic, their script was adapted from the Sumerians.

Chapter Five

Primer Of Impact Of Sumerian Ancient Civilization On Our World

The Sumerians achieved so much largely in part to feeling as if they were a chosen people, and that their success was the will of the gods. On a practical level, Sumerians wanted to improve their daily lives in many ways. All of their advances and inventions helped them develop techniques to increase productivity, which led to the advancement and success of their civilization. All of these beautiful minds brought us so many things: writing for business transactions, schools, agricultural achievements, the wheel, a concept of time that we still rely on, superior metallurgy, a calendar, algebra, and a first set of laws, to name a few briefly.

Although it's exciting to consider each of their contributions to humankind in this primer and in the following chapters, there's one question that needs to be answered first. While we know Sumerians were so beneficial to the development of human civilizations, what drove them? Did they want us to find out about them years later, as evinced by the indelible marks their civilization made on making our lives easier and improving the human experience?

In our search for answers to this question, one can start to speculate based on achieving an understanding of the relationship Sumerians had with their gods. The celebrated Sumerologist Samuel Noah Kramer in "The Sumerians: Their History, Culture and Character," from his all-encompassing thorough studies of the Sumerian culture, came to determine that Sumerians realized that they were part of a larger humanity which inhabited the four *ubda*s (the four regions the world is divided into as a whole). He assessed that Sumerians could not have achieved as much as they did both materially or spiritually without their special psychological drive, which motivated their behaviors and deeply colored their way of life. They were driven by a drive for preeminence and prestige, and for victory and success. In other words, they had a will to superiority. He found it to be a pervading source of motivation for the Sumerians throughout his attempts to piece together evidence from their time.

In his studies of emotional drivers that pervaded Sumerian life, Samuel Noah Kramer found that both fear and love of life permeated their civilization in all its forms and aspects. They also valued material prosperity and well-being. The kings boasted about bringing these to the Sumerian people. Psychological causes for Sumerian achievements make sense to us.

If one of the reasons for civilization was agriculture, then what stimulated their new inventions and organizations? For one thing, it was the ownership of property. Sounds reasonable if you consider that once there was settled agriculture, there was a need for new kinds of laws and enforcement mechanisms, which spurred innovation. When people start settling into their way of life, what is one thing that is a deep need for us? Many would consider security. There are key incentives to stability also. One could imagine that once the Sumerians developed irrigation ditches and sluices they had managed to come a little closer to that sense of security they were seeking. Since they could create surpluses with greater certainty, their drive for stability gave them improved results.

One can easily understand the development of several innovations like the wheel and potter's wheel, as these would increase productivity; it's a key human motivator. With more innovations, a greater variety of tools could be developed to improve the quality of life. Trade by land and sea developed for and motivated by a need to find greater resources, since Sumer itself didn't have as many advantageous resources as its neighbors. Finally, at least in terms of why the Sumerians began to keep lists for a variety of purposes, making order out of chaos drove them. We can relate to that.

In terms of their written laws, the Sumerian proclivity to keeping records of their legal transactions inspired many other civilizations. Did they have a problem that needed to be solved beforehand that led to too many disagreements? Why did they create their written laws? Did the need for agricultural change rather than state formation drive their agricultural and technological advancements? A lot can be determined from the many clay tablets that share their laws and help us interpret how important law and order was to their culture.

Finally, let's return to their relationship to their gods. Sumerians felt obliged to their gods. According to ancient texts, each Sumerian city was guarded by its own god. Humans were considered servants to the gods. In studying their creation myth, which was found on a tablet in Nippur, human-like gods ruled over the earth and had toiled over it until they decided to create man to deal with the labor that was too great for the gods. (More about this myth will be revealed in Chapter 11.) However, in trying to determine the drivers of their achievements, studying these ancient myths and texts reveals that pleasing their gods and avoiding their displeasure drove the Sumerians. Each individual had a special protective deity. The gods directed mankind and ideas were god-given in order to labor over the land and fulfill the will of the gods. Rules and regulations were devised by the gods to make the cosmos run smoothly and effectively and became a list of *Me*s, which were a set of laws to keep the world in order. According to Peter F. Smith's "The Dynamics of Urbanism," Sumerians were driven to fulfill the divine command against inactivity.

Of course, it's a matter of interpretation of which drivers presided over their own self-interest. However, it's fascinating to consider what compelled the Sumerians to create some of these amazing discoveries. A fuller description of these inventions and "firsts" appears later in the book, but for the purposes of a handy primer, here's a page of some of the most essential key discoveries that impact us today.

Origins of Writing, including first libraries and schools – The earliest writing from 3300 BCE involved pictographic script. The Sumerians were the first to develop a written language. By 2800 BCE, the script had evolved into signs, which represented syllables; his newly-evolved written language had signs for roughly 600 syllables. Scribes wrote by pressing a writing stick called a stylus into a soft clay tablet. Since the symbols appeared like wedge shapes, their writing is called cuneiform, which means, quite literally, "wedge shaped." The earliest known dictionaries in the world developed when literacy began to spread to the neighboring kingdom of Mari and people needed to translate words in Sumerian into Eblaite, since Ebla was a major educational center. Trade and economic necessities were likely the biggest motivators for writing.

The Wheel – The invention of the wheel, wheeled vehicles, and wheeled tools made the manufacturing of goods easier. It also led to the creation of the chariot, which allowed the Sumerians to be successful in times of war.

The Plow – The simplest plow that was invented broke up the earth so that the farmer could drop seeds by hand into the ground. Then, in the third millennium BCE, newer plows combined both tasks.

12-month calendar, 24-hour day, 60 minutes, 360-degree circle – As an agrarian civilization, their sense of time was shaped by the cyclical nature of seasonal change. They subdivided the calendar into lunar months. They calculated a lunar year's length, which is close to our own. When they developed writing, they found it possible to keep the calendar and predict seasonal changes. We still use the Sumerian sexagesimal system when we divide a circle into 360 degrees or an hour into 60 minutes.

First set of laws – The Sumerians were the first people to make laws to protect people's rights. The rulers made sure that the laws were followed. The earliest known written code of laws was created under the rule of the King of Ur, Ur-Nammu, in about 2100 BCE.

Bull, Lion and Scorpion constellations – These constellations were passed down to our day, as the oldest astronomical cuneiform texts come from the second half of the second millennium BCE. These texts record the Sumerian names for these constellations. Sumerian game boards and vases suggest that they may have originated as early as 4000 BCE.

Irrigation – Cooperation between large-scale settlements led to irrigation, although it was considered a matter of the state under their Department of Public Works thanks to the need for full-time engineers and reliable construction. It led to economic surplus and the ability to trade. Adapting to best exploit the changing aquatic circumstances through irrigation enabled the Sumerians to develop stable agriculture and invest in hydrological control, instead of following the patterns of the shifting waters.

Sailboat – The Sumerians invented a sailboat in order to sell goods along the Persian Gulf and for travel on their rivers.

First to Pave Streets – The oldest streets discovered in Sumerian cities of Ur have been dated to 4,000 BCE.

Asphalt – As early as 3000 BCE, relics unearthed by archaeologists demonstrated the Sumerians used liquid asphalt as a cementing medium or binder for attaching small objects or ornaments to sculptures, carvings and pottery. It was also mixed with clay to form dense mastic for casting molds.

First to have created clay envelopes that led to the postal system – Sumerian bureaucrats made clay envelopes to hold clay tokens. Tax collectors made these clay tokens to represent various goods like bushels of grain and livestock to tally the actual goods they had collected. The impressions on the side of the clay envelope of the tokens acted as a tally of the goods. Additionally, the Babylonians used the clay envelopes when they began their own postal systems.

Glass – The Sumerians pioneered the early use of glass. Although the exact location of glassmaking is uncertain, archaeological evidence suggests Sumerian archaeological sites have yielded lumps of raw glass and glass objects as early as the twentieth and twenty-first centuries BCE. Glass drawings and casting methods are believed to have been used by the Sumerians more than 5,000 years ago. Glassmaking instructions have been found in instructions and glass beads and cast pieces have dated back to 3500 BCE.

First magnifying glasses – Rock crystals, which were cut and polished to the shape of plano-convex glass lenses, have been found. Sumerians had learned how to use the rock crystal as a magnifying glass. It explains how they could have read some of their own inscriptions on tablets since the cuneiform is very tiny (less than a few millimeters high).

First flushing toilet and a complex sewer system – Sumerians built sewers under cities. They had a complex system of sewers and flush toilets with pipes of baked brick.

Uniformly accepted system of weights and measures – As a commercial people, the Sumerians introduced the world's first uniformly accepted system of weights and measures informally at first until usage and tradition fixed their values. We'd like 1 manu (18 oz.) of barley please!

First to brew beer – Sumerians loved *"kash,"* their word for beer that was as thick as porridge. While some reviews suggest that the beer may have been actually alcohol-free, hard evidence of their fermentation process and beer production dates back 5,000 years, including unearthed ceramic vessels from 3400 BCE. One 4,000 year old seal bears a a Sumerian "Hymn to Ninkasi," the goddess of brewing. The hymn is a recipe for making beer and it is the earliest account of (1) combining barley, baking bread, (2) crumbling it into water to form a mash, and then (3) making it into a drink. It is recorded as having made people feel "exhilarated, wonderful and blissful." It was considered a divine drink and a gift from the gods.

Urban Planning – Sumerian city-states became the world's first urban centers.

Chapter Six

What Did They Look Like?

We gain an understanding of what the Sumerians looked like from their sculptures. In the field of art, they were noted for their particular skills. According to acclaimed Sumerian scholar Samuel Noah Kramer, the men either were clean-shaven or wore long beards and long hair parted in the middle; likewise, women often parted their hair in the middle, then braided them into pigtails and wound them around their head. In terms of fashion, the women often wore elaborate headdresses and dresses, which looked like shawls, revealing only the right shoulder. Men often wore a long felt cloak over a flounced skirt or a chiton (a long skirt). Women often wore head coverings. When they wore sheepskin skirts, the skins were turned inside and the wool was combed into decorative tufts and pinned into place. Sometimes, these tufts were extended to the knees or waist, and if it was someone of great importance, then the tuft may go to the ankle.

Their fashions did change over time. Apparently, in 2500 BCE woven woolen fabric replaced the sheepskin look, although the tufts remained. During the summer months, wealthy women wore yellow, orange, green and scarlet loose-fitting long gowns. While wealthy men wore the short wide skirts like a kilt and a fringed shawl over one shoulder, poorer men and women wore simple knee-length tunics. When the temperature dipped, men and women both wore animal skins.

Sumerians wore wool since they raised goats, sheep and lambs, according to historian Nadia Kirkpatrick in "The Sumerians." Men and women probably wore leather sandals, while soldiers are depicted as wearing boots. Sumerians also grew flax and wove its fibers into linen clothes. They wore jewelry; women wore beads and pendants and rings made of ivory, gold or silver and makeup. They also used perfumes and body oils. If a woman was wealthy, she may have stones such as topaz, lapis lazuli, or carnelian. If it were a more formal event, it was customary for Sumerians to shave the head and wear a wig for a festive occasion when they wanted to look their best, according to "Figurative Language in the Ancient Near East" published by the Hebrew University. The reason women shaved their head and wore wigs was to keep free of lice. Priests were most likely to wear wigs.

According to Jane Shuter in "Mesopotamia," forensic archaeologists who studied the skeletons at Sumerian burial grounds say that they were short and solid. They had thin lips, straight thin noses, and eyes that sloped downward. They suggest that Sumerians were dark-skinned, dark-eyed and dark-haired. As mentioned earlier, the Sumerians referred to themselves as "the dark-haired people."

Chapter Seven

What Shaped Their Worldview?

In understanding their place in the universe, Sumerologist Samuel Noah Kramer analyzed ancient Sumerian artifacts including their literature and myths, with the results being some important contributions to helping us understand the worldview of the Sumerians. For one thing, Sumerian thinkers did not have an exaggerated confidence in man and destiny, as they were firmly convinced that man was fashioned from clay and created to serve gods. Sumerians thought that uncertainty was most common in man's life and that they were haunted by insecurity. As a result of not knowing what the gods might bestow on man, they invested little comfort or belief in free will. In other words, by accepting their dependent status on the gods, then the individual feared his god, but had more confidence in the gods overall than her or she had in earthly matters.

Since man would die despite his or her guardian angel, the Sumerians figured they had good reason to be anxious and perplexed about death and the world below. Sumerian ideas about death consumed their myths and arts. For one thing, they had a gloomy view of the underworld, according to Harriet Crawford in "Sumer and the Sumerians." Based on evidence, there is the impression that their condition in the underworld reflected their social status on earth, not their virtue. Goods that people took to their graves were considered comforts that they could take with them into the afterlife. When a king died, people who worked for him and many of his possessions were buried with him, including wagons and animals.

Given what various Sumerologists have revealed about Sumerians' idea of the nether world, it seems very earthly. The Sumerians thought that after the sun set, it continued its journey through the nether world at night where it turned its night into day. They thought that the moon spent its time away on the last day of each month in the nether world. They did however develop a concept of heaven and hell.

The Sumerians believed to a certain extent in predestination as evidenced by Sumerian inscriptions. They refer to the "tablets of fate of the gods." Sumerians believed that the gods had the power to direct the world. Still, a person could have personal power, with the help of gods, in guiding his current undertakings. As explained by Bruce Trigger in "Understanding Early Civilizations: A Comparative Study," since some Sumerian deities were referred to as the lord or lady of the element of nature that they animated, the whole of nature manifested a divine power that was greater than any kind of power of living humans. Since human destiny was determined in large part by divine powers that manifested themselves in nature or were nature, humans had little say about what would happen to them; nature, and their concept of the deification of nature, played a major role in shaping their social order.

Learning more about these deities involves being open to the idea of gods that had both human and animal attributes, which for some in modern cultures may demand a departure from familiar practices or thought. However, in broadening our understanding of the Sumerians, it is useful to understand that nature was not regarded as divine, but as places where divine power might manifest itself. Deities might convey messages to humans through natural events. This is why these deities needed to be worshiped with rituals, sacrifices and prayers. Since the god that was manifested in a certain object or place decided whether they would cooperate or not with humankind, then humans needed to understand this when say, flint chose to flake so it can become a tool, or if it cracked rendering it useless, as Craig Eisendrath mentioned in "Beyond Permanence: The Great Ideas of the West."

One could embrace the possibility that the Sumerian worldview made earth a divine estate and man its caretaker, since the gods had made humans from clay, as will be further discussed in Chapter 11. The Sumerian King List proclaimed that kingship descended from heaven first to the city of Eridu and then later after the Great Flood to the city of Kish. City-states had to be administered on behalf of their own local god. Given that Sumerian literature explores their belief that the gods to relieve themselves of toil created man, then they believed that men literally fed the gods. No light task!

Since human beings were passive, the council of men who held power in the city-states paralleled the power of the council of gods who determined the order of nature and the occurrence of events. Therefore, the divine council ultimately decided a person's fate. In pursuing their achievements, they did nothing on their own, but were using the talents that were given to them by the gods only to achieve it through the work of their own personal god (as mentioned earlier, each individual had their own personal god similar to a guardian angel). Therefore, being an autonomous individual did not shape the Sumerian worldview as it does many people in modern cultures.

Even given the number of inventions and ways that the Sumerians began to control the world around them and utilize nature for their own advancements, Sumerians continued to understand that their temporary and passive role in society could not lead to being god-like in the sense that life ends for humans. There was no point then to defy the gods or challenge them for the power that Sumerians imbued the gods with since, humans are vulnerable to life's changes.

One might have considered based on the Sumerian agricultural way of life that their worldview would be very close the cycles of life. Daniel Lockwood in "Unlikely Heroes: Ordinary People with Extraordinary Faith" argued that their worldview was based on a cyclical view of reality. Since life was seasonal, predictable, and deterministic, human experience plods along and human beings are mere pawns in a divine drama with no hope for progress or change. This worldview is often compared to biblical views of life, where humans are seen more as participants in their own history and takes on more of an optimistic view than that of the Sumerians.

When considering their attention on trading agreements, an interesting study of the Sumerian gods and their symbols interprets the choice of symbols as transcending the confines of Mesopotamia. Maria Eugenia Aubit in "Commerce and Colonization in the Ancient Near East" considers that because the system of symbols and iconography were common from Iran to Syria, this undoubtedly facilitated the establishment of trading agreements between territories despite long distances. Does this suggest that Sumerians saw the world as an opportunity to connect with other humans despite their identity as Sumerians? Symbols are considered a universal human process. Cultural anthropologists consider that by creating symbols, human beings have created a way to tie themselves to other civilizations or other groups. In fact, the shared meaning of symbols enables people to interact with each other with the least amount of ambiguity and misunderstanding. If Sumerians had some idea of a pan-Asiatic worldview, more research will be necessary to reveal this.

However, their concept of the human situation was very mythopoeic and inconsistent, unfocused on resolving the reason for why a righteous man would be beset by a prolonged series of misfortunes and disasters for apparently no reason. According to Jaroslav Krejčí in "Before the European Challenge: The Great Civilizations of Asia and the Middle East," Sumerians appeared to behave in such a way that they could recognize whether the grace of the gods was with them or not. In other words, they accepted the whimsical rule of their gods without complaining too much about it or questioning it. They spent a good portion of their time placating them, but, since they didn't have much to look forward to when their souls departed their bodies - and their gods didn't provide great role models for morals and values – the Sumerians focused more on breakthroughs in technology and practical knowledge.

One other contributing factor that shaped their worldview has to do with their agricultural life and their business sense. According to Thomas Cahill in "The Gifts of the Jews: How a Tribe of Desert Nomads Changed the Way Everyone Thinks and Feels," the Sumerians weren't just looking at the world through a theological, philosophical lens, trying to answer the big questions about humanity and its struggle. They were practical, down-to-earth businessmen, who were most interested in calculating the extent of their fields and warehouse capacities. They developed an economic dependence to achieve their end means and pursued trade, leading them to develop the first sailboats and to pursue intercultural knowledge sharing and trade relations. International relations shaped their worldview. The materials that their growing economies required needed to be imported from different places and increased trade with local mountain areas provided stone and timber. Traveling to regions as far away as Oman, Cyprus, and the Danube River was a necessity. Sumerians invested a lot of energy into commerce to produce urban goods they felt were vital to their culture. Archaeologists discovered an Uruk-period warehouse that is "literally brimming with objects made of imported woods, precious and semiprecious stones, and metals," according to Michael C. Howard in "Transnationalism in Ancient and Medieval Societies: the Role of Cross-Border Trade and Travel." However, while the Sumerians took on a mindset of consumers of imported goods and agricultural suppliers, they did not play a primary role of being directly involved in actually conducting the long-distance trade.

Their enduring concerns over time lend perspective to human's search for meaning, accomplishments, progress, and ways to improve the quality of our lives that, despite our differences, transport us to their time and transcend the gulf between our own cultural rites and rituals and theirs that do not speak to us today.

Chapter Eight

How Did They Survive?

Sumerians built their collection of city-states. The first city was Eridu, widely considered the first city in the world. It was the capital of the Early Dynastic Period. Since Eridu was the site of a small shrine during Neolithic times, it grew into a large temple on a platform during the course of the fifth millennium. During the Sumerians' Early Dynastic Period (2900-2334 BCE), they shifted from priest kings (*ensi*) to more modern day concepts of kings. Eridu was reputed to be the earliest city of all, the home of the god Enki who saved humankind from the flood. Sites during the Ubaid period that preceded the Sumerian civilization at Ur and Eridu were small. Ur was built around 4000 BCE and was a prosperous city by 2800 BCE.

Remote-sensing studies have shown that these areas were predominantly marshland. As mentioned in "Handbook to Life in Ancient Mesopotamia," by Stephen Bertman, the climatic changes that had begun in the middle of the fourth millennium BCE had originally affected the north. They then persisted to affect the south where the Sumerians were by drying up the rivers and streams and making arable land scarce. The Sumerians started solving these problems by building their networks of irrigation canals and a centralized authority in order to achieve the excavation and maintenance quality required. The disputes for water rights led to armed conflicts and the rise of one city-state over another.

While the precise timing of the first urban growth remains a matter of debate, the Sumerians started to transform Uruk during the period covering the entire fourth millennium BCE. It was a time of rapid and important change, characterized by the first use in metallurgy of alloys like bronze and casting processes, the introduction of the wheel in pottery, and the introduction of pictographic writing on clay tablets. It has been deemed somewhat of a revolution result-wise, although the process was a lengthy one. The number of interrelated factors that went into this period of human development vary and include the development of import and export trading, based on the ability to successfully store surpluses of goods, irrigation, efficient economic developments and protections, geography, and increased population.

Although the Uruk period is often a celebration of their highest achievements and it was one of the most powerful of all of the Sumerian city-states, the cities that flourished during the Early Dynastic Period include Kish, Isin, Nippur, Shuruppak, Lagash, Larsa, Ur and Eridu as well. The Early Dynastic Period gets its name from the fact that each of these cities was governed by royal dynasties. The rise of the First Dynasty of Lagash occurred in 2500 BCE. Eventually, Sumerian conflicts between city-states were regulated by the pantheon. Nippur played an early role in dispute mediation. Some degree of normative regulation between the city-states did exist with procedures instilled for boundary disputes, like the water conflicts mentioned earlier. Sumerians would end up putting a premium on centralized order during the shifts and conflicts of their civilization.

As villages and towns developed into cities, then cities turned into centers of trade, cultural centers and seats of political power, global trade developed. But how did they manage to survive and what was daily life like for a Sumerian? It seems that the Sumerian population actually included Sumerian and Semitic ethnic elements, although most of the diverse people shared the Sumerian material and daily culture.

The average Sumerian house had several rooms with six-foot thick outside walls with no windows to keep the houses cool. Early houses that dated back to about 3500 BCE were huts made of mud and reed. Gradually, they built their houses with mud-bricks. Evidence shows that their Early Dynastic Period houses were equipped with hearths and/or ovens. They had storage jars set into the floors. Some had bread ovens. The Sumerians developed a use lime plaster to coat the clay structures and increase their strength and aesthetic appeal. Architectural elements for Sumerian houses often incorporated central courtyards as well.

According to plant remains found in tombs, their food could have been varied, but the staples were unleavened bread, fish, dates, and a variety of vegetables. Remains of pigs, goat, and sheep were found in royal graves, as well as chickpeas, crab apples and fish. Beer was a common drink according to Sumerian texts, consumed through long straws from a communal jar. Foods varied depending on class and social status. Temple workers had a staple of barley, beer and fish, while the better-off had access to such things as date-wine.

Sumerians used millet, wheat, and barley in their bread and cakes. They also used barley for their porridge, or ground it down to make flour for a flat bread. They also enjoyed stews. Sumerians may have used sesame oil and honey. When they caught fish, they speared them. Sumerians liked pork and they had special butchers in charge of preparing meats. They ate birds, wild boar, deer and gazelles as well. As their city-states evolved, people could get their food from bazaars, including various fruits and vegetables, cheeses, spices, and meats and fish. They preserved their foods for leaner times by drying meats, fish and crops. Although not everyone produced their own food, a structured system of distribution, measurement and exchange was developed. They also tracked food distribution. Crops also included olives, flax, grapes, and beans.

Given the importance of farming, the Sumerians developed new technologies as the need arose. These included stone axes, grinding stones, digging sticks, sickles, hoes and threshing boards to separate grain from husk. Animal-powered plows simplified soil preparation and planting. Once they advanced in metallurgical works and in irrigation, Sumerians became even better suited for large-scale agriculture. Taxes were collected on food and valuable items. Since the Fertile Crescent was known for its dry summers and wet mild winters, it was the perfect growing environment for wild grains.

When we consider what the Sumerians perceived as threats, one significant development, that of the acquisition of land, wealth, and food, gave rise to threats of theft and raiding local or neighboring inhabitants. According to the National Geographic Society's "Edible: An Illustrated Guide to the World's Food Plants," these new threats generated the need to build walls around settlements. It also led to the development of weapons and defense-oriented armies.

In the previous chapter, the Sumerians' worldview appeared pessimistic with little human capacity to improve the way that the human struggle could empower them. Bruce Trigger, in "Understanding Early Civilizations: A Comparative Study," explains that the constant threat that the Sumerians faced as a result of natural catastrophe, intercity warfare and foreign invasions was reflected in their pessimistic view of the way in which the gods managed the universe. Brian Todd Carey, Joshua Allfree, and John Cairns in "Warfare in the Ancient World" remind us that as the number of Sumerian city-states grew and expanded in the third millennium BCE, new conflicts arose as city-states fought each other for control of local resources. They also had to unite at times against the persistent threat of barbarian raiding and invasions. As one can imagine, and not just how the era is depicted in popular culture such as at the movies, the Sumerians began to build walls to surround their city-states as a practical measure to augment a sense of security and protect their citizens.

As they built their city-states, they assigned each city-state under the rule of a local god or goddess. Narrow lanes separated small crowded houses. Each of the cities was built around the shrine of the local god. The temples were elaborate and stood on raised platforms. They created architectural wonders that are Sumer's most characteristic contribution to religious architecture called *ziggurats* (literally: holy mountain), which were temple towers with circular staircases or ramps around the outside. They consisted of rectangular central shrines and were surrounded on its long sides by a number of rooms that the priest used. Ziggurats were the largest buildings in the area.

Aside from the technical accomplishments of building their city-states, the Sumerians built their societies with pride and felt that their city life made them superior to others. Their patriarchal societies were complex. They developed a social structure that was hierarchical with an upper, middle and lower class. Mostly, common people grew dependent on the nobles or priests for their survival given the threats that the city-states faced. Women had rights and some managed to become financially independent. They did retain slaves; these included captives taken in battle or criminals who were treated as personal property, but mostly fairly. As laws took shape, there were limitations and protections put in place. The trade networks they developed may have been some of the first in world history with significant consequences. The number of merchant clay tablets that reflect receipts and business transactions have led most experts to determine that the purpose of learning how to write and the origin of writing was economically motivated.

Family life was a central part of Sumerian culture and tended to be very close knit. People often lived in large family groups. When a child reached marrying age, parents arranged their marriages, as it was considered a practical arrangement, although there is evidence of some being motivated by love and desire. Love between friends was not as strong as love between blood relations, according to a Sumerian proverb. A contract was signed at the time of marriage between the man getting married and his father-in-law rather than his future wife. Many couples came to love each other, even if they barely knew each other or never met before their wedding day. Their family life has been seen as evidence of freedom, harmony, and a sense of duty; they accepted by doing the right thing even in the case of divorces or massive familial conflicts.

While Chapter 9 will focus on their leadership, one very valuable contribution that the Sumerians made towards improving their society was the establishment of what are considered to be the first comprehensive set of laws. While many extol the Code of Hammurabi as the earliest known record of laws set forth by a government, that isn't necessarily true. The earlier laws of Ur-Namma (or Ur-Nammu) (Code of Ur-Nammu ca. 2112-2095 BCE) of the twenty-first century Ur III period is the first full set of written code found, and is the oldest surviving tablet containing a law code that was written circa 2100 BCE. However, Urukagina, who reigned as the ruler of the city-state of Lagash circa 2380-2360 BCE, is credited as providing the first example of legal codes in recorded history, as he combated corruption and created laws that reformed the practices of the rich of the city towards the poor and orphans. Documents reveal the history of man's struggle for freedom from tyranny and oppression, including bitter struggles for power between temples and palaces. Urukagina targeted his reforms toward abuses of power, including seizures without right or warrant of property. He was supposedly chosen by the god *Ingirsu*, the deity of the city, to reestablish divine laws that banned many horrible practices that had gone unchecked.

Under Ur-Nammu's rule, during what was considered the Sumerian Renaissance after the Assyrian King Sargon had briefly conquered Sumer before his empire fell, laws were written 300 years before the Code of Hammurabi. Archeological remnants of legal records recording deeds of sale were found dating back to 2700 BCE. Some of the laws that were created under Ur-Nammu settled arguments between individuals and some gave justice to the poor. Since Sumerians valued family, Sumerian family law indicated the punishments and protections meted out to those who were involved in marital disputes, incest, parent-child disputes, inheritance, adoption and disinheritance. Laws also dictated marital relations with slaves (which were permitted), marriage arrangements, slave rights against a master, children's rights, children's debt responsibility of a parent's failed payments, divorce, adultery, sale of daughters and sons as slaves, slander, and the abolition of certain taxes. The laws generally compare favorably with those of other primitive peoples in regards to the treatment of women.

The law was the moral ideal, as to obey these laws was to worship the will of the gods, who were considered the authors of the laws. Sumerians thought that promises meant a lot, given the number of contracts existing to this day, and they prized being law-abiding individuals. That's not to say they were always successful with their ideals of justice and truth. Concubinage was a legal institution; while monogamy was an ideal, polyandry was practiced, even in the wake of an inscription during the reign of Urukagina that the ruler denounced women with multiple husbands. There were prostitutes, and sexual intercourse with a slave girl or prostitute had negative connotations. Sumerian women were victims of violence, including rape, assault and battery, and murder.

Sumerians did have established holidays. They had holidays to celebrate "The Month of the Eating of Barley of Ningirsu," "The Month of the Eating of the Gazelles," and "The Month of the Feast of Shulgi." They made special sacrifices and held processions. They held regular monthly feasts on the day of the new moon, the seventh, fifteenth and last day of each month. They celebrated the New Year's holiday (which took place in March) in grand style over several days with special feasts and celebrations. They held a rite, which was a holy marriage between the king and one of the priestesses, to ensure the fecundity and prosperity of Sumer and its people. The biggest religious festival the Sumerians had was a celebration of fertile soil and growing crops called the festival of Akiti. It was usually held every March at harvest time.

The marketplace was the center of activity where Sumerians gathered to trade their wares and talk about the day's news. Traveling merchants, farmers and local merchants exchanged with locals gathering to make their purchases. Sumerians loved beautiful objects. Families and clans often taught crafts. There are early records of jewelry workshops and large workshops for metalworkers, goldsmiths, stonecutters, leather workers and various craft trades. They shopped in stores that were at the center of the Sumerian political power structure. Besides merchants involved in large-scale trade, Sumerians set up as shopkeepers and peddlers who sold to individuals. Reference to "a merchant's leather bag for weights" is evidence on a clay tablet, among many others, that document their merchant activities. Sumerian transnational relations were not occasional; long-distance trade on a regular basis was of significance. The contribution of trade to enriching the lives of Sumerians played a large role in their culture and helped shape a society with a great division of labor, and promoting the rise of the cities with populations that exceeded 10,000 occupants.

Retail merchants were held to a very high standard; dishonest practices were not tolerated. There are even records showing house-to-house small traders. According to "Daily Life in Ancient Mesopotamia," Sumerians had a word meaning "specialist" for those who were specialized at craftsmen skills. Their artisans made pottery, tableware, and jewelry with skill. Sculptors carved small statues, sometimes of gods and sometimes representing humans.

They were highly developed at music. The Sumerians developed a harp and a lyre. The oldest existing stringed instruments are a handful of beautifully made Sumerian lyres that have survived. They also played lutes, a variety of wooden flutes, reed pipes, and percussion instruments. The lyre is first depicted on Sumerian art works about 3000 BCE as resting on the ground and standing higher than a seated person. Music was important in the temple; singing and instrumental music were important in religious ceremonies. Eleven highly ornamented instruments have been found at Ur. Music was also an important part of civic life. Many cuneiform tablets that have been studied relate to tuning and playing instruments and include scales. Their musical system was exported at least as far away as the Mediterranean coast and it is likely that ancient Greeks learned Mesopotamian music theory and math in the Near East. The octave was known, based on analysis of the instruments. In addition, their hymnographies were a highly sophisticated art form that included dirges and elegies.

The majority of Sumerians were farmers, cattle breeders, boatmen, fishermen, merchants, scribes, doctors, architects, masons and carpenters, smiths and traveling merchants. Even the poor had their own farms and gardens. Private property was the rule rather than the exception. Nobility owned most of the land. While Sumerian society was exposed to the interconnectedness of tribalism and urbanism at work, in urban environments where creativity, invention and freedoms for women were more apparent in both work and private lives, the tribal societies had different ways of seeing the status of women and crime. Tribal customary laws upheld the dominance of men over women, and although by the first millennium many vestiges of tribalism had been forgotten, it was a vast clash with urban societies. In regards to crimes, tribes that settled into cities were not accustomed to systems for the administration of justice, as crimes were dealt with within the tribe, clan or family. The differences in the two cultures played out as the city-states grew.

While Sumerians originally began to write for the purpose of deeds of sale of property, sales, inventory, and institutionalizing relations between private interests and the city-state, writing later turned toward myth, religion and literature. After it was a technical matter, writing brought with it lists of goods that became a general theme of their culture. It is doubtful that when they invented writing, they imagined it would be used for anything but administrative needs, with writing history, literature and science texts far from their minds. According to V. Gordon Childe, a professor of Prehistorical Archaeology at the University of Edinburgh, under the conditions that the Sumerians had, writing was a difficult and specialized art that had to be learned by a long apprenticeship, with few possessing either the leisure or the talent to penetrate the secrets of literature. Scribes were a restricted class.

The conditions Childe mentions include the fact that the clay tablets were heavy and not suitable for movement. They required temple scribes for deciphering. The writing that was done for administrative purposes was enforced authoritatively at one central place over a small area given these conditions. In fact, Samuel Noah Kramer suggests that access to the writing culture was probably given only to a small number of the population, so there was likely a small reading public. The ability to write itself possessed an authority of its own, and might have seemed like magic or a supernatural ability. This would have boosted scribes into the upper class.

Of course, once the Sumerians did begin to write literature and myths, some of them have become classics – like "The Epic of Gilgamesh," a text that many study in undergraduate literature classes today. Sumerians were the first to develop epic literature consisting of heroic narrative tales in poetic form. From the fragmentary sources of Sumerian literature, many are religious in character, but Sumerologists do not characterize them as written exclusively by priests. Studies of these works suggest that there is no sense of climax, with little intensification of emotion and suspense as the stories progress and no attempt at characterization and psychological delineation. Their literature seemed to be mostly for the purpose of praise. The magical power and use of praise was used to instill the virtues presented in the praise. The praise poems were written for kings. Their myths revolved around love, as in for example, "Inanna's Descent to the Nether World – Queen of Heaven."

However, one can also show cultural appreciation for their wisdom compositions that included argumentation, detailed farmers' almanacs, and proverbs.

Rite and ritual played a predominant role in their culture, with the temple at the center of these practices. Sumerian traditions include temples that held an overarching importance within the cities in Sumer. They were the dwelling places of the city-gods and the cities grew around them, extending back as early as the Ubaid period. Socio-economic and political authority stemmed from these houses of god. Early rulers were expected by tradition to have assumed ruling status over the communities through a close connection to temples and claimed to be sanctioned by the gods. The Sumerians anthropomorphized their gods through an established canon of sculptural representation from Early Dynastic times. Their deep-seated religious traditions, social structures and concepts of decision-making, and leadership shaped much of what emanated from their culture.

The Sumerian scholastic tradition grew and developed as the earliest known dictionaries in the world were conceived when literacy began to spread from Sumer to neighboring kingdoms like Mari and Ebla. Ebla scribes and Sumerian teachers worked together in Ebla, the ancient city of Syria, at a major educational center. As the origins of literacy grew, Sumerian schools and education improved the quality of life in city-states and allowed for an exchange of knowledge that was unprecedented, becoming a time honored tradition for Sumerians. The

Edubba (Sumerian school for youth) became important and integral to Sumerian life. The scribes began to think in terms of teaching and learning. Textbooks emerged, dating back to 2500 BCE. Professors and teachers wrote essays to introduce school life. In relating to their tradition of education, we can find that worries of their school children were similar to modern worries in terms of misbehavior and attitudes. Scholastic achievement wasn't easy, but it was a tradition that was now firmly established by the Sumerians.

The Sumerians were also known to be into sports, and these activities figured into their social traditions. There is hard evidence of jugglers, wrestlers, and tumbling acrobats taking part in the festival for *Ishtar*, the Sumerian goddess of love, fertility and war. Wrestlers are depicted in statues and upon seals and stelae, and described in administrative documents and epic poetry. There are also administrative records that describe city runs. There is evidence from circa 2600 BCE of a game that can be compared to field hockey called pukku-mekku (ball and stick). Physical performances at their festivals were quite common. Sumerians placed considerable emphasis on the human body according to inscriptions, art, and administrative documents that have been unearthed.

As a culture, the Sumerians created a system of elaborate language and writing, architecture, arts, astronomy and math. Chapter 10 will discuss further the results of their cultural desire to achieve so much and leave their mark on humankind. Urbanism was the defining characteristic for large numbers of Sumerians and helped preserve long-established traditions of social relations, kinship and family structure. Domestically, social conditions altered very little across time. The importance of traditions played a central role in the formation of the daily lives of Sumerians, but so did the way they developed their cities, governing bodies and their ethos for achieving the most that Sumerians could by pleasing their gods and their will toward superiority in all of their endeavors overall. Of course, their writing tradition allowed for the scribes of the kings or travelling merchants to expand their inter-city and international relations. The Sumerians built a cultural and empire-building tradition that established their place in history and was modeled regularly by humankind.

Chapter Nine

Kingdoms, Dynasties And Notable Events

"Man is the shadow of god, but the king is god's reflection."

—*A Sumerian proverb*

Early city-states had a king who was assisted by noble officials and priests in ruling their domain. Kings were often considered figureheads of the priests, although they did exercise decisive power over time. It is figured that the first rulers were probably priests. The Sumerian word for high priest was *en*. Behind the priests stood the immense power of the high Sumerian gods who were the deities of sky, fire, earth, salt, storm and water. The city was ruled by the elite headed by the king. In Sumerian, a palace was called an *égal* (great house) or *élugal* (house of king) and a temple was called an *édingir* (house of a god). A king was called the *lugal*. As mentioned earlier in the book, during their Early Dynastic Period (2900-2334 BCE), by many accounts it is believed that they shifted from priest kings (*ensi*) to more modern day concepts of kings as *lugals*, which is now construed to mean hegemon.

The concept of kingship was grounded in religion, and kingship was invented by the gods as the most effective means to govern themselves. Struggles for supremacy among the major cities continued throughout their history. The infamous Sumerian King List, which has mostly been preserved, was written about 2100 BCE and contains a list of all the kings of the regions and their accomplishments; it also includes high amounts of mythological hyperbole and links the kings to their gods. Therefore, it has been the task of Sumerologists to sort through this list to determine fact from fiction. However, it is still considered one of the greatest sources of information on Sumerian rulers. It also lists the lone female monarchy, Kubaba, who held the throne in the city-state of Kish around 2500 BCE. Certain excavations have reoriented skeptical attitudes toward the King List, given that the evidence supports some of the claims that were made in it. It also reflects old traditions within a chronological framework. Derivatives of the King List have also been found, although no two of these is has proven to be identical.

The list explains that kingship was considered a divine institution and talks about the great floods, like the Bible does during the times of Noah. It lists the kings who reigned before the flood and excites researchers, given the window it opens into the past. The list's value has been a subject of debate, but many experts see that it influenced politics in its day, impacted various literary compositions and chronological recordkeeping, and inculcated a particular political vision. The king list describes several dynasties, which Sumerologists now consider ruled simultaneously. It also does not list all the dynasties.

The power of the *lugals* became great as they were elected as the leaders of war and to solve the problems that civilians faced. Once the Nippur League developed to deal with the conflicts across city-states, this alliance between these cities handled the constant raids along their northern and western borders by nomads who took much of the Sumerian lands. The constant conflict led to the permanence of the *lugals* as war leaders, and dynasties formed. During the Early Dynastic period, the first major king of Sumer was Etana. He founded the dynasty at the city of Kish and was the first ruler to unite the separate city-states. During the Heroic Age (2650-2550 BCE), the King of Kish, Menbarragesi (2630-2600 BCE) disarmed the Elamites to the east of Sumer. Thereafter, the dynasty of kings of Erech, Ur, Kish and Lagash vied for ascendancy for hundreds of years and rendered Sumer vulnerable to external conquerors. He was said to have been overthrown by King Gilgamesh of Uruk.

The most famous Sumerian king is undoubtedly Gilgamesh. The "Epic of Gilgamesh" is one of the world's oldest surviving pieces of literature. The Gilgamesh of the epic was probably the same Gilgamesh who ruled the city of Uruk during the first half of the 3rd millennium BCE. He was the fifth king of the first dynasty of Uruk. Although the tales of his feats and his rule prevail, we know little about his actual achievements. He is considered to have ruled around the twenty-seventh century BCE and may have been the one who led to the building of Uruk's mighty walls. In the epic of his quest for immortality and fame, he rejects his humanity and wants what the gods have, explaining why his journey is so important. He was known to have conquered nearby cities. He overthrew the rulers at the city of Kish, shifting power to the city of Uruk. Harriet Crawford in "The Sumerian World" writes that only the rulers of Uruk, like the famous Gilgamesh, seem to have used *en* as a royal title. Scholars consider the *en* to have more of a priestly role than the lugal. Did he establish his authority in such a way as to make the Sumerians consider Gilgamesh as either considering himself too much like a god, or that the Sumerians saw him as more godlike than other kings? The questions linger.

While the Sumerian city-states held political power and vied for ultimate primacy within Sumer, extension of a city's political power did occur a few times in the history of the region. Some of the city-state rulers were able to establish control over neighboring people. Lugal-Anne-Mundu, the ruler of the city-state of Adab in the 2400s BCE. was the most famous of the kings to extend his power beyond the Sumerian lands. He is sometimes credited as establishing the first empire in history, according to Michael C. Howard in "Transnationalism in Ancient and Medieval Societies: the Role of Cross-Border Trade and Travel." His desire for control of Elam, Subartu, Guti, and the Amorites may have had to do with their valuable resources. The towns of northern Syria that prospered in providing Sumerians timber, stone, metals and wine from northern Syria, Lebanon and Anatolia were in his sights - Lugal-Anne-Mundu was prompted by their generated wealth to invade the area, despite the fact that there was mostly peaceful commerce in the region, not conquest. However, his empire collapsed when he died, and these regions reasserted their independence.

The rise of the Akkadian Empire occurred under the reign of Sargon the Great (2770-2215 BCE). Sargon conquered the Sumerian city-states and a couple of Elamite cities as well. He was credited for creating the world's first multinational, centrally-ruled empire, as it stretched across the majority of Mesopotamia. After Sargon's rule, the Sumerian kings were praised for the order they provided. The collapse of the Akkadian Empire during this time led to increased attacks by the nomadic Amorites.

The king of Ur, Ur-Namma (or Ur-Nammu) (2112-2095 BCE) is a prominent figure as a king, because he became the king of Sumer and Akkad after Sumer reemerged as an independent entity once the Gutians had swallowed it up into the Akkadian Empire in 2150 BCE. He gained many victories against the Gutians, united the Sumerian cities into a single nation, and reconquered Akkad. He had reversed the roles, making the Sumerians the rulers after a 200-year period characterized by Sumerians existing as vassals to the Akkadians. This time was considered the Neo-Sumerian Revival as well as the apex of Sumerian civilization. Ur-Namma promulgated the first law code of man's recorded history. His father, King Utuhegal (2133-2113 BCE) had also been an important Sumerian ruler, as he had used the death of the Gutian King Simm to attack the Gutians, which had initially restored Sumerian power. Yet Ur-Nammu is considered to have restored the ancient state of affairs by re-establishing Sumerian rule, formulating regional alliances to thwart the growing power of the Amorite nomads in the Syrian steppe. He died in battle fighting the Gutians. A rare royal inscription that was found describes the defeat and death of the king in battle.

However, one more prominent king, the son of Ur-Nammu, Shulgi of the Third Dynasty of Ur (circa 2094-2047 BCE) carried out a punitive campaign against the Gutians as well as an expansionist policy. He was at war on a regular basis, clashing with Hurrian invaders, and oversaw the construction of a wall to keep the Amorites out. He proclaimed himself a divinity and established a tradition of royal praise for himself in temples which included many hymns. According to Harriet Crawford in "The Sumerian World," Shulgi himself had been trained as a scribe. He boasted about this training, set up scribal schools and introduced new weights and measurements. He also presided over a huge expansion of the civil service. This was unusual for someone who was destined to be a king, as scribes were considered an instrument for controlling the image of the ruler and shaping historical memory. By some accounts, in 2088 BCE, during what is known as the King's Run, documents show that Shulgi claimed that during a celebration of *eshesh*, he ran the distance of the parade (200 miles round-trip) from Nippur to Ur and back; while it might not be true, it would have been possible based on an analysis of the diet available, water available, climate and topography. His alleged run could also have been part of the practice of using imagery to bolster royal kings, to portray them as heroically brave and very strong, in order to embellish the king's virility. By all accounts, according to William Hamblin in "Warfare in the Ancient Near East to 1600 BC: Holy Warriors at the Dawn of History," Shulgi was a superb athlete. However, during his reign, the Amorites captured him and carried him away in 1750 BCE.

By 1750 BCE, King Hammurabi, one of the kings of the Amorites, ended the Sumerian civilization and started the history of Babylonia, a Semitic state built on a Sumerian foundation. The fall of Sumer forced former Sumerians to migrate. Sumerian soon was no longer spoken aloud, but it was written, although it was mostly replaced by Semitic Akkadian. As mentioned previously, Hammurabi is well known for his codified set of laws for all of Babylon.

Throughout history, Sumerian kings signed treaties with neighboring states. Some of the most prominent sculptural art pieces of the time depict military triumph, such as the Stele of Vultures, which depicts the ruler of Lagash's victory. The Stele of Vultures was commissioned by Eannatum, ruler of Lagash (circa 2450 BCE) to celebrate their victory over Umma. These treaties were made in the name of their gods. As a ritual, oaths were considered so important to keep that if there was a known violation of a treaty, it entailed a curse and punishments. Wars were frequent and interests clashed. When one city made war upon another, it was considered by the Sumerians that the cause of it was that their gods were feuding. The notable treaty between Lagash and Umma handled the perennial civil war between the two city-states. It is considered the best record of the world's oldest boundary treaty contained in a cuneiform pronouncement and refers to the original border treaty between Umma and Lagash dating back to 2550-2600 BCE. Some Sumerologists estimate that the treaty itself records earlier boundary agreements that occurred dating back to 3100 BCE. It can be viewed at the Louvre Museum in Paris. The Stele of Vultures derived its name from the sight of vultures feeding on the bodies of the 3,600 dead Umman soldiers. The god of Enli had revealed how to settle the dispute to the king of Kish, who then proceeded to act as an arbiter and made the decision binding.

Sumerian armies often came into conflict with foreign states, including the northern cities of Ebla, Mari and Asur. When it came to Sumerian conflicts between city-states, Nippur, the home of the council of the gods, played an early role in dispute mediation. Procedures were used to settle boundary disputes. The king's duties included leading the military, overseeing trade and judging border disputes. Numerous tablets have been found relating to these disputes. Cities governed over hearings and issued warnings that had to do with building or agricultural disputes, safety issues and civil law. Courts and the legal codes handled disputes surrounding property, civil matters and crimes. While Chapter 10 will discuss the advancements made in weaponry making, it appears that ancient history relied on all manners of conflict resolution, including mediation, arbitration, treaties and writing, all of which simplified at least the procedural aspect that may have led to resolutions. While mediation may be one of the most common forms of dispute resolution in intergroup relations, wars were not always averted and internal and external threats persisted.

Chapter Ten

Major Contributions To Humankind

One of the most thrilling and significant excavations of Sumerian artifacts occurred in 1902-1903 when the existence of schools dating far back as the 25 th century BCE was proven. Excavators found the earliest school texts from Fara near Uruk. The German expedition under the direction of archaeologist Robert Koldewey also found economic texts that included sales of houses and fields, indicating that private ownership existed in Sumer; however, the Fara lexical texts carried great importance. The Sumerian school was called an "*edubba*" or "tablet house." While schools were generally thought to only have the purpose of training scribes originally, Sumerians developed other areas of study for wealthy boys including writing, math, religion, zoology, geography, grammar, language, forms of legal and administrative documentation and geology. Girls learned domestic arts and went to music schools, but there is no evidence of women ever becoming scribes. Poor children often went uneducated, being needed to attend to their family's farm or work in their father's shop.

An "*ummia*"("school father" or "expert") headed the school. Teachers were called "big brother" and students were called *dumu edubba* or "school's son." Memory exercises were emphasized, as students would recite their studies to the class. Whips were used to encourage students to work harder and to maintain order in the classrooms. A statuette of a schoolmaster from Lagash known as "Dudu the Scribe" was found, apparently a real man who had lived in Lagash around 2500 BCE and dedicated the statue of himself to *Ningirsu*, the city god. Semitic children also had to learn Sumerian. Private schools became established when literacy spread beyond the confines of temple and palace administrations, especially among some craft workers and merchants. According to Sumerologists, schools aspired to be centers of learning where old texts were copied and preserved and new ones composed. A student would memorize tablets that were prepared the day before, study them, and copy them. Later, the *ummia* examined their tablets. Practice tablets have been found filled with exercises.

By all accounts, scribe schools were not easy. Students attended from childhood until graduating as a young man and school days were notoriously long. Upon graduation, a young scribe was in great demand by royalty, merchants or anyone who needed documentation. They surveyed land, managed estates, acted as judges and settled arguments and claims. Language was the most important subject. Since trade played such a central role in the Sumerian culture, scribes needed to learn to understand them. They would memorize word lists and phrases.

Although education wasn't universal or compulsory, after training, students could call themselves *dubsar* or scribe, becoming a member of a privileged class. Once a student learned all the basic cuneiform signs, students went on to learn thousands of vocabulary words

Agricultural

Sumer is considered an important early farming society. Agriculture is one of the two greatest transitions in human history, with the other being the Industrial Revolution of the eighteenth and nineteenth centuries. More than 90% of the tens of thousands of clay tablets unearthed in the region are economic and administrative, including accounts of agriculture and other industries. Sumerians gave us the ox-drawn plough, getting food from intensive agriculture, and riding in wheeled vehicles. They were the first to build wheeled carts and wagons. They invented the potter's wheel to create bowls and greatly improved farm production.

The Sumerians are widely known to have devised irrigation systems to deal with the inadequate rainfall in the region. As a necessary measure, they developed these techniques to use water from the Euphrates. They invented basin and shadoof irrigation methods in order to channel water to agricultural fields and for human consumption in their cities. They also invented hoes, sickles, and constructed dykes.

Since Sumerians could forecast weather patterns, this helped them plan their farming activities. As a result, they developed the lunar calendar. With surplus agricultural products, this led to job specialization and the development of trade. They are considered to have developed a quite modern invention when they made the seeder or machine planter. The way the machine worked is clearly shown in an illustration from about 1500 BCE. A Sumerian didactic composition "Instructions to a Farmer" that has been preserved gives step-by-step advice on how to conduct a model farming operation in cereal culture. Although some people think that pesticides are a modern invention, Sumerians used elemental sulfur to protect their crops from insects. The first recorded use of this sulfur was used to control insects and mites by 2500 BCE, according to Mark Winston in "Nature Wars: People vs. Pests." The rise of agriculture and the use of irrigation and farm equipment marked a revolutionary change in the journey of humankind and allowed for the world's first cities to thrive.

Architectural & Urban Planning

Sumer's most characteristic contribution to religious architecture is the ziggurat. It was the most important building in the city, and built on a high terrace in its center. Constructed by using straw to reinforce sun-baked bricks, ziggurats were almost like a city unto themselves; they contained shrines, homes for the people working in the temple, storehouses, and magazines. Sumerians also introduced mud-brick columns and half columns. In the city-state of Erech, Sumerians developed the unique method of ornamenting the mud-brick walls and columns with clay cones (or decorative pegs) dipped in different colors. The Sumerians employed arches, domes, and vaults to give the impression of grandeur and space and devised decorated walls.

Additionally, leaving behind the reed huts of villages, Sumerians invented planned, patterned architecture. They took marsh reeds and bound them into columns and arches. Later, these reeds were plastered and decorative pegs would be installed as well.

With regard to urban planning, Sumer is the site of the first city-states (Eridu and Uruk). Sumerians built sewers under cities. They had a complex system of sewers and flush toilets with pipes of baked brick. As the first to live in cities, Sumerians developed urban planning methods that became somewhat of a yardstick to other city-states; their urban planning and craft of government has given us historical insight, as we look at the developments in human history.

Astrological & Numerology

Sumerians believed that the changing skies could influence human behavior. It was considered the premier means of divination for ancient Mesopotamians. They believe our destinies were written in the skies, according to Stephen Bertman in "Handbook to Life in Ancient Mesopotamia." Joseph Farrell in "The Philosopher's Stone: Alchemy and the Secret Research for Exotic Matter" wrote that although the exact origins of astrology are not known, it was present in most advanced civilizations of antiquity including the Sumerian civilization; he advances the possibility that in particular most contemporary Western astrology stems from Sumer. Sumerian records show that they recorded their astrological observations on clay tablets and then interpreted them from an astronomical point of view. He and others who study the field of astrology consider all of this speculative, since it is unlikely a specific date will ever be tendered for the appearance of astrology. However, Stephen Bertman revealed that after the Sumerians named all the constellations (the names we still call them by today), in the fifth century BCE, astrology took a personal turn. While astrologers had focused on determining astrological divine signs for kings and the fate of nations, it became the first time that services were offered to ordinary clients. Suddenly, given evidence in the form of inscriptions and clay tablets, astronomers were hired to provide sketches of the zodiac with astronomical explanations to try to predict a child's future based on birth dates or presumed dates of conception.

According to Richard Gabriel and Karen Metz in "From Sumer to Rome: The Military Capabilities of Ancient Armies," Sumerian medical knowledge during 1700-1200 BCE was corrupted by the rise of a mystical numerology that strongly colored their medical practice. Those who study numerology consider that the Sumerian numerical system led to Chaldean numerology, which predicated that numbers were linked to the energy of the universe and moved in the divine order of things. According to those who are in the field of this ancient mystical science involved in the study of numbers, Sumerians, Akkadians and Babylonian numerology endowed numbers with meaning and mysticism in parallel with the mathematical skills of their civilizations. For psychics, astrology and numerology go hand in hand, as astrological charts and reading require certain calculations, this renders astrology dependent upon numerology as they refer to one another.

So what's your sign?

Biblical Parallels

A Sumerian precedent exists for the Nook of Job, and as Sumerologist Samuel Noah Kramer observed, "it represents man's first recorded attempt to deal with the age-old yet very modern problem of human suffering." In his book, "History Begins at Sumer," Kramer also credited the Sumerians with the "The First Noah," "The First Moses," and "The First Tale of Resurrection," among other biblically related firsts. There are several historians and Sumerologists who have speculated about significant parallels. Although there is exhaustive research on the topic, a few highlights are notable. The Sumerians had the word Eden in their language and scholars have suggested that it may have been adopted from the Ubaidians. One of the Sumerian paradise myths about a land of plenty called "Dilmun" may have been that paradise. Dilmun is described in the myth known as "Enki and Ninhursag" as being turned into a paradise when Enki gave it the gift of water. Additionally, there are Sumerian creation stories that have striking similarities to the story found in

Genesis. Finally, the Sumerian version and Biblical versions of the Flood story show numerous parallels.

Literacy

The Sumerian societal contributions of initiating attempts at becoming literate with some of the earliest known dictionaries in the world made them extremely important in studies focused on the origins of literacy. While access to the writing culture was probably a small percentage of the population, there were different levels of cuneiform literacy. Since the Sumerians created the basis for written language, they recorded everything from taxes, to harvests, prayers, laws, letters, allocations of rations to workers, and scientific observations. They recorded crops that were harvested and stored and distributed. It advanced their ability to build schools and teach on a variety of subjects. Cuneiform is the world's first system of writing, and as the use of cuneiform grew, writing began to be used for academic purposes rather than just for economic and administrative necessities.

Literary

Literature was not intended for a wide audience, but for the royal collections and school libraries for the purpose of study and teaching. The earliest *Epic of Gilgamesh*, which is the most famous Sumerian literature, dates back to the late third millennium BCE. Other versions in Old Babylonian and Akkadian followed. This particular piece of literature had a wide circulation however, since a fragment of the epic tale from the fifteenth or fourteenth century BCE was found in Israel. A large majority of Sumerian literary works is poetic form, without meter and rhyme. Ultimately, the various cultures exposed to Sumerian literature, mythology and writing adopted and adapted these forms as well asthe Sumerian techniques of making books. "The Literature of Ancient Sumer," a 400-page anthology from the Oxford University Press, and presents the most comprehensive collection ever published covering the literary heritage of the world's oldest literature. It contains different types of translated compositions and shows how the study of literature has evolved over the last 150 years. Much of Sumerian narrative text is considered to represent less in the way of narrative and is more about transmitting an idea of Sumerian history and heritage through these stories, poems and hymns. Hundreds of literary tales have survived, including mythological tales, lamentations, and praises of kings and gods in the form of hymns.

Mathematical & Astronomy

The Sumerians developed a formalized accounting and numbering system to record the details of daily and long-term activities. Algebra was used primarily to measure plots of land. They used their mathematical skills for bureaucratic purposes, but as they were also charting the course of the night sky and developing a calendar, it became a necessity. They employed a sexagesimal numbering system which could be counted physically using the twelve knuckles on one hand and the five fingers on the other hand, which creates 60 when multiplied together. Slanted markings represented numbers up to 10. Vertical markings represented tens and multiples of ten. The number 60 was represented alongside these markings. They used different size reeds to record numbers in the tens versus numbers in units of 60 and 600. We continue to use the sexagesimal system since we continue to use 60 seconds in a minute and 60 minutes in an hour, as well as 360 degrees in a circle. Several theories have been explored as to why they chose a sexagesimal system, including one that is based on weights and measures, which divided commodities into thirds (a fraction system). The most popular theory is that it is based on celestial events. Since they named and identified the zodiac made up of seven planets, divided the stars into 12 constellations, and may have considered that the sun moved about one degree per day to get around the heavens relative to the stars making the sum of 360, all these numbers were either multiples or fractions of the number 60.

The Sumerians accomplished a series of firsts. They were the first to make the mathematical calculations to predict the future position of certain planets. They were the first to calculate that the square of the hypotenuse of a right triangle is equal to the sum of the squares of its other two sides. There is evidence from between 2500-3000 BCE of multiplication and division tables, tables of squares, square roots and cube roots, geometrical exercises, and a complex system of measurements. There is evidence of many financial obligations written on tablets that are expressly seen as loan contracts. According to Marc Van de Mieroop in "The Origins of Value: The Financial Innovations that Created Modern Capital Markets," usually tablets were soaked in water so the clay could be reused. Therefore, once a financial obligation was settled, the documents were destroyed, explaining why there are likely only a fraction of tablets remaining of those once written. The Sumerian word for interest was *máš*. In the sexagesimal system of weight measures, the mina and shekel were two basic units. The mina was sixty times larger than the shekel.

While there are some fascinating reviews of the various interest rates that Sumerians placed on different commodities, loans with interest are thus first attested to Sumerians and were a constant feature of their financial system until the end of the cuneiform documentation in the late first millennium BCE. Their use of the terms loans and interests were similar to present use. Their invention of interest and loans spread out all over the Near East by the third millennium, except for in Egypt.

In terms of advancements in astronomy, the Sumerians made star catalogues and used a 12-month solar calendar along with a 354-day lunar calendar. By the 3 rd millennium BCE, they regularly used a 360-day calendar. Evidence found in the underground library of King Ashurbanipal in Nineveh has puzzled experts, since it may indicate that the Sumerians observed the impact of an asteroid over 5,000 years ago. Drawings of the constellations as astronomical animals appeared on cuneiform texts and on the earliest occurrence of these motifs on prehistorical seals, Sumerian vases and gaming boards. They developed astronomical mythology and provided us with Constellation names like Leo, Sagittarius and Capricorn. They mapped the movement of the sky, sun, stars, planets, and moon. Their trackings were based on spherical geometry. They drew diagrams and measured distances on their charts to determine possible distances in space. Scholars who study Sumerian myths consider that the myth of *Inanna*, the Queen of the Heaven, is a direct reference to the movements of the planet Venus when it disappears near the Sun for a period of time. They predicted sunrises and settings that were accurate enough to predict eclipses. They kept accurate tables that predicted the future position of celestial bodies based on mathematical formulas.

Medical

The oldest known therapeutic manual comes from Sumerian history. According to Jo Ann Scurlock and Burton Anderson in "Diagnoses in Assyrian and Babylonian Medicine: Ancient Sources, Translations and Modern Medical Analyses," they were among the first to appreciate the advantages of a recorded medical tradition. The manual dates from the Ur III period (2112-2004 BCE) and contains instructions for the treatment of patients without diagnoses. Physicians used polished rock crystal that could have been used for closer examination of skin and other tissues. Scurlock and Anderson determined that it is no exaggeration to say that the skill of ancient Mesopotamians in diagnosis and therapy was only surpassed in the late nineteenth century CE.

Thousands of Sumerian tablets dealt with medicine, science and mathematics, myths and fables. The types of cuneiform tablets that pertain to medicine can be divided into omen collections or symptom texts, medical texts or therapeutic, and informative texts on diseases and practices. Illness was regarded as a divine punishment for sins and required both practical and spiritual healing. The Sumerians were the first to separate the clinical practice of medicine from the control of the priesthood, which allowed for medicine to be practiced independently from magic and ritual. Sumerians had two kinds of doctors: the *asu*, who used practical herbal medical cures, and *ashipu*, who used magical cures. The oldest known written collection of prescriptions dates back 4000 years.

Folk medicine and primitive medicine attempted to rid their patients of disease-causing demons. Ancient medicine found plants and herbs to be important. Medicine and herbs were essentially equivalent. According to Lois N. Magner in "A History of Medicine," medications are said to have been tested or discovered by unimpeachable authorities and patients considered it prudent to attack a disease with a combination of medicine and magic. According to Richard A. Gabriel in "Man and Wound in the Ancient World: A History of Military Medicine from Sumer to the Fall of Constantinople," the Sumerians invented the first standards of medical ethical conduct with set statutory fees for physicians and penalties for malpractice.

The first evidence of a military medical corps in the armies of the ancient world confirms that physicians regularly attended the army in the field and remained in the rear of the battle. There is some evidence that Sumerian doctors used distillation pots to make chemical compounds, and if that is the case, then they were the first medical practitioners to make distilled compounds for treating wounds or ailments. As early as 3000-4000 BCE, the Sumerians seem to have cultivated opium poppy and applied it for general anesthesia for painless surgery. It was referred to as *hulgil* meaning the "joy plant" and the art of poppy culling continued in the region.

According to Charles Kahn in "World History: Societies of the Past," the Sumerians were also the first to depict medical treatment of animals in a reference to a cattle doctor on a tomb wall built between 2200-2000 BCE.

Transportation

Improvements in land and sea transportation helped move people and products over longer distances and fostered trade networks. The invention of the sailboat improved the ability to move food surpluses during harvest as well as import demanded goods. Experts consider the invention of the wheel the first known mechanical device. While ancient Mesopotamians had reed boats before they had sails, the rudimentary boats and paddles were no match for these sailboats, which were quickly put to good use and enabled the Sumerians to participate in the kind of commerce they needed for a thriving economy. Cloth sails were known to the Sumerians at least by 3500 BCE. It was the first time in history that some source of energy available in nature was successfully harnessed to do a type of work, according to Harold H. Schobert in "Energy and Society: An Introduction."

Weapons

The Sumerian invention of the chariot ranks among their major military innovations. Both the wheeled chariot and bronze weapons became increasingly essential as individual city-states fought for supremacy. Before 3000 BCE, Sumerians learned how to make weapons by smelting copper with tin to make bronze. They created socket axes for close combat. Their sickle-sword was a precursor of the sword, which was derived from an axe. Their primary long-range weapon was a composite bow and sling. Then, they developed a penetrating axe and a shaft hole axe.

Books have gone into depth on these and various aspects of Sumerian life, taking a deeper look at attempts to piece together the fragmentary evidence to broaden the picture of human history through their records. Many titles are included at the end of this book to foster your further exploration.

Chapter Eleven

Religion & Myths

Since the will of the gods affected all Sumerian settlements and ruled over nature and humanity, the Sumerians attributed much of their success and accomplishments to pleasing their gods. The Sumerians were very similar to many agrarian civilizations in that they believed in a host of nature gods. They were polytheistic; each city-state had its local god that needed to be appeased and that determined the prosperity of the citizens. Kings often had priestly roles. Each individual had their own god to whom they prayed and who gave the individual blessings.

If we look at their concept of the structure of heaven and earth, we get a sense of Sumerian cosmology and how they associated these realms with their gods. Their term for universe was *an-ki,* which is a compound word meaning heaven-earth. The earth was a flat disk and was enclosed by a surface in the shape of a vault. *Lil* was the substance between heaven and earth, which means, air, breath and spirit. It corresponds to our atmosphere. They viewed the sea as a prime mover and never asked themselves what preceded the sea in time and space, according to Sumerologist Samuel Noah Kramer. When heaven and earth were separated by the atmosphere, astral bodies, animals, plants and human life were created.

The gods were manlike in form and needed to feed themselves, marry and support themselves, but were superhuman and immortal. They were also prone to human weaknesses and passions. They lived on the mountain of heaven and earth where the sun rose. Male and female deities had specific competencies in natural and human matters. *Innana* was the goddess of love and fertility. *Enki* was the god of water, wisdom and creation and from his loins (the Sumerian word for semen is the same as water) sprang most of the deities that gave life to the world. He oversaw the making of the first human, fashioned out of clay, and is often the one who was called upon to resolve conflicts. *Enlil* was considered to be one of their most important deities, as he was the air-god. He was known as the father of the gods and gave kingship to kings and rulers. Other important gods included: *An* (the god of heaven), *Utu* (the god of the sun), *Nanna* (the god of the moon), and *Ki* (the goddess of the earth).

While Sumerian priests and holy men developed a complex set of rites, rituals and ceremonies to placate the gods, the scribes, poets and bards created a rich mythology. Singing and chanting were considered to have healing powers. It wasn't just astronomers who studied the stars, as priests and priestesses studied them, in additional to people's dreams, to predict the future. Sacrifices were practiced, including human sacrifice. When the well-respected excavator Sir Leonard Woolley arrived at the site of Ur in 1922, he discovered the Royal Graves of Ur outside of the ziggurat. While ordinary graves contained a body wrapped in matting or placed in a wood or clay coffin, the Royal Graves had elaborate burial chambers and were distinguished not only by the wealth accompanying the dead but the array of human sacrifices, which included the attendants of the royal personage, either drugged or poisoned before burial. However, an examination of the skulls from the royal cemetery in 2009 suggests that more gruesome sacrificial methods were used including sharp instruments and that death ensued from blunt-force trauma. Sacrifices in the name of the king played an essential role in providing the gods what they needed. Generally, sacrifices that did not have to do with the death of a royal person took place in the temple and were offered on occasions such as feast days.

One Sumerian ceremony has revealed that in the city of Ur, the religious rituals of the moon goddess *Nanna* brought king-priests closer to the gods when they mounted their ziggurats to reenact the drama of the gods unfolding in heaven. According to Daniel Lockwood in "Unlikely Heroes: Ordinary People with Extraordinary Faith," ultimately Sumerians yearned to sway the divine cycle just enough to earn a fertile crop season and a year of pregnant wives. The Sumerians believed their cities were created by the gods and goddesses. In "Ritual Sacrifice" by Brenda Ralph Lewis, offerings and sacrifices were justified, as it was Man's destiny to act as servants to the gods. They sacrificed animals, burnt incense and aromatic woods, and gave the divine portion to the gods, while the feast participants would eat the rest. Offerings could include leaving divine property at the temples, like boats, chairs, drinking vessels and other exotic offerings like jewelry. If someone was ill, then models of the part of the body that was suffering from disease or disability were left in the temple so that a cure could be granted. Human sacrifice was in a category of its own and was not a regular practice. It was considered a last resort or, as mentioned, part of mass burials of a royal household.

According to the Sumerian creation myth that can be found on a single clay tablet found in Nippur from approximately 5000 BCE, the creation of Earth, " *The Eridu Genesis*," it appears that Enki is the main god. It is one of the oldest extant creation stories and one of the most famous. After the universe was created of the primeval sea and the gods were born, the deities made man from clay found in the ground. After cities were built and kingship was instituted, the gods decided to destroy humanity, but Enki did not agree with the decree and commanded that a boat be built. It is one of several flood references found in the dozens of civilizations worldwide. The flood was referenced in the Sumerian King List and records pre- and post-flood kings.

Finally, according to Sarah Iles Johnston in "Religions of the Ancient World: A Guide," the history of Mesopotamian religions offers a complex picture. However, it must be stressed that the basic structure and ideology of Mesopotamian religion was largely Sumerian in origin. The book offers a very detailed, informative look at Mesopotamian religions. The purpose behind many of the Sumerians' achievements has many links and ties to their religion and myths, given that their myths and religion taught them subservience to their gods and that they discerned the cosmic order of the universe at the mercy of willful powerful cosmic forces identified as gods and goddesses. Thus, their insecurity would cause them to create as much order as possible to build their own civilization, given that Sumerian theology assumed that order was designed into the cosmos at its creation by superhuman and immortal beings that governed the order and tasked humankind to keep it established.

Such a philosophical approach would explain the relationship between humankind and nature even at the time of Sumerian civilization. The relationship was one that necessitates harnessing the power of the natural world for the achievement of the human creators of cities, agricultural industries and trade empires in order to promote the venerated cosmic order. They did it the only way they knew how, through applied engineering, science and humanities. Perhaps in developing our views of the world today, we might not base our views on the same held beliefs of the Sumerians. However, we do find that it is uniquely human to continue to make sense of our human experience; while the methods and answers might vary in understanding, we can accept a uniquely human place in the world.

Conclusion

Extreme changes over recent decades in the fertile lands famous for the world's earliest cities and the life of our early human ancestors appears to be threatening to vaporize the ancient Sumerian and various Mesopotamian cultures whose secrets still lie deep below the surface. While much study has been done to decode and translate the life and times of the Sumerians, ongoing studies continue despite desiccation of the Mesopotamian Marsh in Iraq and political instability in the region. Closing in on understanding the uniquely human attempts of navigating ancient times without the preponderance of modern tools and the availability of vast knowledge intrigues us, not just because we can learn from their lives and discoveries but because it sheds light on the human experience and our shared commonalities of interests.

Even as the world's media focuses on Syrians fleeing violence and terror in the region, many of us have turned our attention to Mesopotamiato better understand the nature of conflicts now.

However, building on all the excavations to date is a significant human interest that has some foreboding challenges. For one thing, scientists determined in 2001 that the rich Fertile Crescent was almost gone, based on satellite imagery; only 10% of the important ecosystem still remained. In 2009 Aki Hitoh, a meteorological forecaster of Japan's Meteorological Research Institute in Tsukaba, Japan, assessed that the ancient Fertile Crescent will disappear in this century and that the process has already begun. Iraqi ministers have conducted urgent talks about the drought and tensions over water dams that have negative consequences on preserving the region. Farmers have been abandoning the Fertile Crescent.

In early 2016, Popular Archeology magazine published a cover story about how the culture in the Fertile Crescent was likewise drying up. The passing of Sumerian knowledge systems to the Ma'dan people, the culture of the Marsh Arabs living there, and traditional ways of life will soon be lost, according to the authors. The Ma'dan culture is tightly interwoven with the ecosystems of these marshes. Some farmers believe that the drying out of the region touched off the social turmoil that burst into the Syrian civil war, leading to the refugee crisis; climate change hastened the civil war. Copious reports and much media attention has tried to report on how the Fertile Crescent may cease to exist.

The Global Seed Vault in Svalbard operated by the Norwegian government, also known as the Doomsday Vault, has preserved seeds that have been grown by humanity for years. They include the important storehouse gene bank in Aleppo, Syria that includes over 100,000 varieties of crops inherited by previous generation, both extinct and existing. The Aleppo center has sent a good portion of the seeds and samples to the Doomsday Vault as backup.

To add another terrifying dimension, Daesh (ISIS) is deliberately destroying antiquities. At the National Museum in Damascus, Ma'amoun Abdulkarim, the director of antiquities and museums, has described how gloomy his job has become when talking to Smithsonian Magazine in March 2016, highlighting the negative psychological effects of hearing about the destruction of antiquities. This museum also safeguards tiny clay cuneiform tablets developed by the Sumerians, which they explain to museum visitors was among the region's many transformative contributions to history and culture. Abdulkarim believes that while people in Syria are concerned primarily with matters of life and death, worrying about antiquities means also understanding that they are from these different past empires and civilizations, including the Sumerians, Assyrians, Akkadians, Mongols, Arabs, Persians, to name but a few. Syrians feel the threat to their shared inheritance intensely. It's a blow to their hybrid identity forged by all of these ethnic and religious groups, and is considered incomparable.

The race to save antiquities is on for all of humanity. Recent research from the Museum of the Sealand into the Sumerian past explains how the Sumerians made the Amorites pay for a wall they built to protect themselves from their neighbors. Currently, Iraq's newest and most ambitious museum slated to open by September 2016 will have collections of artifacts from ancient Sumer, Babylon, Assyria and Islamic periods of Iraq's history behind steel doors. The museum inhabits the site of former Iraqi ruler Saddam Hussein's residence. Last year, archaeologists at the Slemani Museum in Iraqi Kurdistan announced they had found fragments of a tablet detailing 20 new lines of text from the *Epic of Gilgamesh*. It is considered a timely reminder of just how precious archaeological and historical heritage from the Middle East is and how the wars and disorder - particularly involving Daesh - are a threat to all of humanity's cultural inheritance.

One of the most exciting current excavations happening is in Ur, Iraq. According to National Geographic in March 2016, the joint US-Iraq team reopened excavations in the city of Ur (an ancient city-state of Sumer) in the fall of 2015, an endeavor supported by the National Geographic Society. After uncovering a modest-sized building dating to a couple of centuries after Ur's peak, senior Iraqi archaeologist and area native Abdul-Amir Hamdani said, "This is typical Iraqi housing." He added, "There's continuity in the way people live here." Their assessment helps their team question some earlier archeological conclusions, like the idea that social mobility in city-states like Ur was impossible given that elites controlled the large population of workers. He said that it hints at a society that wasn't under the control of a small tyrannical minority. They've also uncovered a small clay mask of *Humbaba*, a giant who protected the cedars of distant Lebanon mentioned in the *Epic of Gilgamesh*. Their botanical finds are being analyzed to understand how the diet of citizens changed over time. They've also found evidence of Sumerian long-distance commerce: dark tropic wood and a sliver of ebony from India 4,000 years ago. This wood is the first evidence that supports Sumerian texts that mention "black wood of Meluhha." The team has also found a wealth of other exciting finds and will continue to dig deeper in the search for evidence of how the non-elite lived at the height of Ur's wealth and power.

Enduring mysteries surround the ancient city-states of the Sumerian civilization. They help us to continue to question previous thought on interpreting archaeological finds and help find new data relating to the history of Sumer and humanity's shared cultural inheritance. The search continues to reconstruct the story of humanity's past. Given that the Sumerians shaped many aspects of our world with their inventions and early systems, our curiosity continues to lead us down a path to better understand ancient civilizations as we continue the uniquely human trait of making sense of our world for our own knowledge and to collect it for future generations. As humans, besides seeking morality and culture, we pursue knowledge for its own sake and yearn to apply it to improve our circumstances.

As the inventors of writing, Sumerians started to represent the world around them - and that's something our human ancestors would appreciate that we still do today. Despite the language barriers and thousands of years, humans still rely on each other.

Cited Sources and Reference Materials

Amalia E. Gnanadesikan, The Writing Revolution: Cuneiform to the Internet
Volume 25 of The Language Library (John Wiley & Sons, 2011).

Amanda H. Podany, Brotherhood of Kings: How International Relations Shaped the Ancient Near East (Oxford University Press, 2010).

Anne Draffkorn Kilmer, "The Musical Instruments from Ur and Ancient Mesopotamian Music," Penn Museum, Volume 40, Issue 2, July 1998.

Barry B. Powell, Writing: Theory and History of the Technology of Civilization (John Wiley & Sons, 2012).

Brenda Ralph Lewis, *Ritual Sacrifice: Blood and Redemption* (The History Press, 2013).

Brian M. Fagan, The Long Summer: How Climate Changed Civilization
[ACLS Humanities E-Book] (Basic Books, 2004)

Brian Todd Carey, Joshua Allfree, John Cairns, *Warfare in the Ancient World* (Pen and Sword, 2006).

Britannica Educational Publishing, Astronomical Observations: Astronomy and the Study of Deep Space - An Explorer's Guide to the Universe (Britannica Educational Publishing, 2009).

Bruce G. Trigger, *Understanding Early Civilizations: A Comparative Study* (Cambridge University Press, 2003).

Catherine Griffin, Abrupt Climate Change Impacted Ancient Civilizations in the Fertile Crescent, *Science World Report July 24, 2015.*

Charles A. Frazee, *World History: Ancient and medieval times to A.D. 1500* (Barron's Educational Series, 1997).

Charles Kahn, *World History: Societies of the Past* (Portage & Main Press, 2005).

Clara Moskowitz, "Q&A: Dead Languages Reveal a Lost World," *Livescience December 28, 2010.*

Clay Spinuzzi, Tracing Genres Through Organizations: A Sociocultural Approach to Information Design Volume 1 of Acting with technology (MIT Press, 2003).

Claude Reignier Conder, *The Hittites and their Language* (W. Blackwood and Sons, 1898).

Craig Eisendrath, *Beyond Permanence: The Great Ideas of the West* (Xlibris Corporation, 2011).

Craig A. Lockard, Societies, Networks, and Transitions: A Global History (Cengage Learning, 2010).

Daniel Lockwood, Unlikely Heroes: Ordinary People with Extraordinary Faith (Daniel R Lockwood, 2012).

Deane Anderson Lamont, "Running Phenomena in Ancient Sumer," *Journal of Sport History, Vol. 22, No. 3 (Fall 1995).*

Dick Teresi, Lost Discoveries: The Ancient Roots of Modern Science—from the Babylonians to the Maya (Simon and Schuster, 2002).

Don Nardo, Mesopotamia - Exploring the ancient world (Capstone Classroom, 2012).

Dr. Brian Fagan, Chris Scarre, *Ancient Civilizations* (Routledge, 2015).

Dr. Philip Leech, "How climate change threatens the cradle of civilization," *Middle East Monitor April 12, 2016.*

Francis W. Galpin, The Music of the Sumerians: And Their Immediate Successors, the Babylonians and Assyrians (Cambridge University Press, 2011).

Fred Pearce, "Fertile Crescent 'will disappear this century'," *New Scientist* July 27, 2009.

Gil Stein, Rethinking World-systems: Diasporas, Colonies, and Interaction in Uruk Mesopotamia (University of Arizona Press, 1999).

Graham Faiella, *The Technology of Mesopotamia* (The Rosen Publishing Group, 2006).

Hammurabi (King of Babylonia.), The Letters and Inscriptions of Hammurabi, King of Babylon, about B.C. 2200: To which are Added a Series of Letters of Other Kings of the First Dynasty of Babylon, Volume 3 (Luzac and Company, 1900 digitized Dec. 10, 2009).

Harold H. Schobert, Energy and Society: An Introduction, Second Edition (CRC Press, 2014).

Harriet Crawford, *Sumer andthe Sumerians* (Cambridge University Press, 2004).

Harriet Crawford, *The Sumerian World Routledge Worlds* (Routledge, 2013).

Hebrew University Jerusalem M J Geller, M. J. Geller, M. Mindlin, J. Wansbrough, *Figurative Language in the Ancient Near East* (Routledge, 2005).

Historical Encyclopedia of Natural and Mathematical Sciences (Springer Science & Business Media, 2009).

Hraq Vartanian, "Required Reading," *Hyperallergic* *April 3, 2016.*

Gilbert LaFreniere, *The Decline of Nature* (Oak Savanna Publishing, 2012).

G. M. Lees and N. L. Falcon, "The Geographical History of the Mesopotamian Plains," *The Geographical Journal Vol. 118, No. 1 (Mar., 1952), pp. 24-39.*

Jacob Shavit, History in Black: African-Americans in Search of an Ancient Past (Psychology Press, 2001)

James Harkin, "The Race to Save Syria's Archaeological Treasures," *Smithsonian Magazine March 2016.*

Jaroslav Krejčí, Before the European Challenge: The Great Civilizations of Asia and the Middle East (SUNY Press, 1990).

Jane Shuter, *Mesopotamia - Excavating the past* (Heinemann-Raintree Library, 2005).

Jo Ann Scurlock, Burton R. Andersen, Diagnoses in Assyrian and Babylonian Medicine: Ancient Sources, Translations, and Modern Medical Analyses (University of Illinois Press, 2005).

Joan Aruz, Ronald Wallenfels, Metropolitan Museum of Art (New York, N.Y.), Art of the First Cities: The Third Millennium B.C. from the Mediterranean to the Indus

Metropolitan Museum of Art Series (Metropolitan Museum of Art, 2003).

John Wendle, "The Ominous Story of Syria's Climate Refugees," *Scientific American, December 17, 2015.*

Joseph P. Farrell, *The Philosopher's Stone: Alchemy and the Secret Research for Exotic Matter (Feral House, 2009).*

Julia Harte, "In Cradle of Civilization, Shrinking Rivers Endanger Unique Marsh Arab Culture," *National Geographic Explorers Journal April 24, 2013.*

K. Anne Pyburn, *Ungendering Civilization* (Psychology Press, 2004).

Kanishk Tharoor and Maryam Maruf, "Museum of Lost Objects: Looted Sumerian Seal," *BBC News March 11, 2016.*

Karen Radner, Eleanor Robson, *The Oxford Handbook of Cuneiform Culture* (OUP Oxford, 2011).

Karen Rhea Nemet-Nejat, *Daily Life in Ancient Mesopotamia* (Greenwood Publishing Group, 1998).

Karl Moore, David Charles Lewis, *The Origins of Globalization* (Taylor & Francis, 2009).

Leila Avrin, Scribes, Script, and Books: The Book Arts from Antiquity to the Renaissance ALA classics (American Library Association, 2010).

Lois N. Magner, *A History of Medicine* (CRC Press, 1992).

Maria Eugenia Aubet, *Commerce and Colonization in the Ancient Near East* (Cambridge University Press, 2013)

Mark L. Winston, *Nature Wars: People Vs. Pests* (Harvard University Press, 1999).

Michael C. Howard, Transnationalism in Ancient and Medieval Societies: The Role of Cross-Border Trade and Travel (McFarland, 2012).

Michael Mann, The Sources of Social Power: Volume 1, A History of Power from the Beginning to AD 1760 (Cambridge University Press, 2012)

"Money used by Sumerians in Mesopotamia, says expert," *Hurriyet Daily News Jan. 13, 2014.*

Naida Kirkpatrick, The Sumerians - Understanding People in the Past (Capstone Classroom, 2002)

National Geographic News, "Ancient Fertile Crescent Almost Gone, Satellite Images Show," May 18, 2001.

National Geographic Society (U.S.), *Edible: An Illustrated Guide to the World's Food Plants* (National Geographic Books, 2008*).*

N.C. Datta, *The Story of Chemistry* (Universities Press, 2005).

Peter Akkermans and Glenn Schwartz, *Archeology of Syria: From Complex Hunter-Gathers to Early Urban Societies* (Cambridge University Press, 2003).

Peter F. Smith, *The Dynamics of Urbanism* (Routledge, 2013).

Philip J. Adler, Randall L. Pouwels, *World Civilizations* (Cengage Learning, 2011).

Ricardo Duchesne, The Uniqueness of Western Civilization Volume 28 of Studies in Critical Social Sciences (BRILL, 2011).

Richard A. Gabriel, Karen S. Metz, From Sumer to Rome: The Military Capabilities of Ancient Armies (ABC-CLIO, 1991).

Richard A. Gabriel, *Man and Wound in the Ancient World: A History of Military Medicine from Sumer to the Fall of Constantinople (Potomac Books, Inc., 2012).*

Robert E. Krebs, Carolyn A. Krebs, *Groundbreaking Scientific Experiments, Inventions, and Discoveries of the Ancient World (Greenwood Publishing Group, 2003).*

Samuel Alfred Browne Mercer, *Journal of the Society of Oriental Research, Volumes 1-2* (Society of Oriental Research., 1917, digitized June 2, 2009).

Samuel Noah Kramer, *The Sumerians: Their History, Culture, and Character* (Chicago: University of Chicago Press, 1963).

Sarah Iles Johnston, *Religions of the Ancient World: A Guide (Harvard University Press, 2004).*

Sean McGrail, *Boats of the World: From the Stone Age to Medieval Times (Oxford University Press, 2004).*

Stephen Bertman, *Handbook to Life in Ancient Mesopotamia (OUP USA, 2005).*

Steven Wallech, Touraj Daryaee, Craig Hendricks, Anne Lynne Negus, Peter P. Wan, Gordon Morris Bakken, *World History: A Concise Thematic Analysis, Volume One* (John Wiley & Sons, 2013).

The Highway Engineer & Contractor, Volume 1 (International Trade Press, Incorporated, 1919).

Thomas Cahill, The Gifts of the Jews: How a Tribe of Desert Nomads Changed the Way Everyone Thinks and Feels – Volume 2of Hinges of History (Knopf Doubleday Publishing Group, 2010).

Thorkild Jacobsen, *The Sumerian King List* (Chicago: University of Chicago Press, 1939).

V. Gordon Childe, *The Bronze Age* (Cambridge University Press, 2011).

V. Gordon Childe, *"Childe on Writing in Ancient Sumeria and Egypt," New Learning Online Transformational Designs for Pedagogy and Assessment (Childe, V. Gordon. 1936. Man Makes Himself. London: Watts, pp.179-182, 186-189, 229-231)*.

Volker Mrasek, The Not-So-Fertile Crescent: Climate Change Threatens Cradle of Civilization, *Spiegel Online International April 16, 2008.*

William W. Hallo, Origins: The Ancient Near Eastern Background of Some Modern Western Institutions (BRILL, 1996).

William Hamblin, Warfare in the Ancient Near East to 1600 BC: Holy Warriors at the Dawn of History (Routledge, 2006).

Marc Van de Mieroop on "The Invention of Interest and Sumerian Loans," in William *The Origins of Value: The Financial Innovations that Created Modern Capital Markets,* N. Goetzmann, K. Geert Rouwenhorst (Oxford University Press, 2005).

---

[1] Semitic is a subfamily of Afroasiatic languages that includes Akkadian, Arabic, Aramaic, some Ethiopic, Canannites, Hebrew, Phoenician Abyssinians, ancient Babylonians, and Asyrians. Mesopotamia has been proposed as the possible site for the prehistoric origins of Semitic-speaking people. The Akkadians are a Semitic

group while the Sumerians were a non-Semitic group. There is no evidence of cultural tensions that can be ascribed to differing racial or ethnic identities between Akkadians and Sumerians. Semitic languages have striking differences when compared to Aryan languages. Semites adapted Sumerian picture-writing to their own syllabic method of writing and partly as an ideographic system. When used to describe religion, ancient Semitic languages encompass the polytheistic religions of the Semitic people of the Near East and Northeastern Africa. Today, the three main Semitic religions are considered to be Christianity, Judaism and Islam. Non-Semitic languages are often divided into Aryan or Hamitic religions.

Printed in Great Britain
by Amazon

27481061R10066